HEAVEN'S FREQUENCY

Tuning In To The
Heartbeat Of God

MERCY HOUSE
PUBLICATIONS

SHANNA BARBERIO

Acknowledgments

Thanks to my team who helped me edit and proofread the manuscripts—Sheree Carter, Neil Barberio, Mervin Strother, April Foster, Will Dew, Abby Berget, Rachel Fendley, and Joyce Goodman. Your contributions were true acts of love.

Thanks to Augusto Silva for the beautiful cover design, and thanks to HMDPublishing for the incredible interior design.

A special thanks to *Neil Barberio*, my husband, who encouraged me from the moment I told him I had an idea to write a book. He was an awesome partner to bounce my ideas off of, and he supported me when I needed to devote time to writing.

And finally, I thank *God* for telling me to write a book and then giving me the words to put in it. I'll be forever grateful.

Contents

Author's Note

"Write a book." When God spoke this to me, that's all He said. I could have easily ignored these fleeting words, but something inside me leapt with purpose. I felt the urgency on His message, so I agreed. Receiving no further details, I started writing.

To my delight, God showed up every time I was ready to transcribe. He led me to write about positioning and preparing our hearts to receive the Kingdom of Heaven. At certain points His presence was so strong I had to take breaks from typing to worship Him.

Purpose

It's my purpose to help more Christians live in the presence of God. I want you to be so full of joy and peace that your days are filled with laughter and celebration. I'm no more special than the next person, and I'm certainly not without faults. It's just I want to share the practical ways I've learned to draw on the peace and joy of God.

It wasn't always this way. I've dealt with trauma, depression, anxiety, night terrors, rage, and violence during my life. I believe God took me through those trials to the place I am in now, so I could show others the way out. I feel a burden for those who have such turmoil warring within them. But I can testify that Jesus wants to bring victory to your life, like He did to mine.

Take the Climb

Think of this book as a trek that takes us over a mountain before reaching the Kingdom of Heaven. In Chapters one and two we begin the journey by establishing a rhythm to our stride. Chapters three and four introduce a higher level of effort as we slow down to prepare our hearts for encountering more of Heaven. In chapters five, six, and seven we climb to the summit of the mountain where we push to new levels of personal growth.

Once we've crossed over, the splendors of Heaven progressively come into view. In Chapters eight and nine our trek eases as we become equipped with the resources and power of Heaven. Next, in chapters ten and eleven we enter the gates of Heaven and receive its rewards. Finally, in chapter twelve we discover how to keep Heaven with us, even in the storms of life.

You may find that this book will catapult you into your own unique way to relating with God. That's okay. My goal is to inspire you to walk in the fullness of God's love and to live in Heaven while on Earth.

CHAPTER 1

Tuning In

I was hoping to fall this time. It was 2003, and there I was standing in the longest prayer line I've ever seen in my then 25 years of living. Growing up in a charismatic church, I was familiar with the act of people dropping to the floor when the presence of God showed up, but it had never happened to me.

The conference had reached the much-anticipated altar call, and the keynote speaker was praying for each person one by one. They ushered 2,000 people in rows along the aisles in the sanctuary, through the hallways, and into the other rooms in the church. My husband (Neil) and I stood in a small foyer area.

As the preacher worked through the line, I could hear him coming nearer and nearer. Every... single... person prayed for by this mighty man of God fell under the power of the Holy Spirit like dominos. Here was my chance! I was finally going to feel over-whelmed by God's presence.

I had received Jesus at the age of 6, and had experienced God's power before. But never so much I physically couldn't stand! Surely if 2,000 people were falling under this anointing, God wouldn't leave me out. As the man of God approached, my heart raced. People were dropping like flies every time he said, "Fire!"

This is it! This is it! Okay, let's do a heart check. I thought to myself, *Are my sins forgiven? CHECK. Hands up? CHECK. Eyes closed? CHECK. Focused on God? No! I'm thinking about a checklist!* I suddenly heard him yell, "FIRE!" and felt his hand on my forehead. A few moments later I opened my eyes, and to my dismay my husband and I were the only people standing in the room! *REALLY? Two thousand people fell, and we didn't? Figures.* The preacher was already gone from the room along with my hopes for a powerful encounter with God.

Wanting More

I was used to feeling like I was on the outside of God's presence while people around me were touched by His glory. I spent many a prayer meeting crying out to experience Him with little to no reply. I was missing sustained peace and often wondered if something was wrong with me. Sure, there were times when I sensed God, but I wasn't satisfied with a few chills from a worship song.

I wanted God to feel real to me. I kept trying, researching, and expecting to experience the Father as described in the Bible. Whether or not I was actively seeking God, I always hungered for something deeper I couldn't quite put my finger on.

Have you ever felt this way before? Do you feel left out while others seem to hear God and bask in His power? As Christians we believe God loves all of us, but when others can access God's presence more easily, it can be frustrating.

Don't settle for less of God's presence. Only getting by on the bare minimum of His goodness is not what He wants for you. Jesus paid a lofty price so you could live abundantly. Ask yourself, "What am I missing?" and then seek after it. If you're like me, then you don't want some superficial, emotional crumb of an experience. You want an actual sit-down meal with the Father.

After years of frustration, I told myself I didn't need to feel God's presence to be a Christian. Maybe God wants me to be the level-headed person in the room. I mean if everyone falls on the floor overtaken by the Spirit of God, then somebody has to be the designated driver. It's funny how we can talk ourselves into being satisfied with the minimum. I can now admit I was wrong. God wanted me to experience Him in a powerful way too.

My Background

I grew up in a Christian home with parents who often had people over for discipleship, counseling, and deliverance. My dad was big into discipling and counseling new believers. In fact, his last day on Earth was spent at church counseling others and participating in our corporate prayer meeting. My mom is a mighty prayer warrior and teacher of the Word. On those rare Saturdays I woke up early to watch cartoons, I would sometimes catch my mom praying in the dark hours of the morning. My parents taught me the greatest endeavor in life is to pursue God.

The Gift of the Holy Spirit

When I was thirteen, I wanted to the receive the power Jesus described in His last words to the disciples. He said, *"but you shall receive power when the Holy Spirit has come upon you"* (Acts 1:8 NKJV). When the disciples finally received the Holy Spirit, they spoke in what the Bible describes as unknown tongues. I wanted to experience this because Paul said, *"The one who speaks in tongues advances his own spiritual progress"* (1 Corinthians 14:4 TPT).

This heavenly prayer language can be called "unknown tongues," "speaking in tongues," or "praying in the Spirit." Whatever the name, I knew I needed the Holy Spirit with the evidence of speaking in tongues. Being filled with the Holy Spirit had to be important because Jesus told (not asked) the believers to go receive Him.

I read the book *Good Morning, Holy Spirit* by Benny Hinn and it sparked a hunger in me. In the book, young Benny had given His life to the Lord, but discovered there was an additional experience Jesus wants us to have. After Hinn invited the Holy Spirit to fill him, He received power just like Jesus described. The Holy Spirit gave him boldness, passion, peace, visions, words of knowledge, understanding of scriptures, and much more. Along with all this power came a new language too.

> *Then when Paul laid his hands on them, the Holy Spirit came on them, and they spoke in other tongues and prophesied.*
> *(Acts 19:6 NLT)*

> *I thank God, I speak with tongues more than you all.*
> *(1 Corinthians 14:18 ASV)*

One Wednesday night when I was 13, my mom told me to go to my room so she could pray for me to receive the Holy Spirit and the gift of speaking in tongues. She didn't wait for me to object because she discerned I was more than ready. That night we prayed earnestly for about an hour. After no results, she told me to pray on my own for a while. She left, and I kept praying. Nothing happened... nothing at all.

Feeling frustrated I cried. My cry was so heartfelt it started to sound weird, like I had the shivers. Then it got stranger. To my surprise, I realized I was speaking in the unknown tongues mentions in Acts 2. God had given me my Heavenly prayer language!

My struggle was I've always tried to figure the Spirit out. I can now see I was focused on the wrong things that night. My thoughts were tuned in to my tongue, my words, and what my mouth was doing, so I missed it. Something changed when my mind gave up and my heart released what was inside of me; I began to flow like a fountain.

It's usually the smarty-pants people who have the hardest time receiving the baptism of the Holy Spirit. That night I overcame my problem when I stopped analyzing with my mind and started trusting with my heart.

Revival in My High School

Fast forward 3 years and I was still struggling with being numb to the Spirit. Even though I was filled with the Holy Spirit, I found it difficult to sense His presence on a regular basis. I longed for a deeper connection to God.

I went to a Christian high school in the 90s. During my junior year, the teachers brought a video for our chapel time. It was a recording of Alison Ward at the Brownsville Revival. She was shaking under the power of the Holy Spirit and urging people to repent, because of God's loves for us. (You can find this video at https://youtu.be/4aix9SLcLrE "Brownsville Revival Testimony")

It was hard for me to watch. My parents taught me about demons and deliverance; so, when I saw people shake my paradigm said, *That's a demon. God wouldn't make people shake.*

As I watched, I recognized what she was saying was Biblically true. *Why would a demon tell us to repent?* Fortunately, I decided to not be totally closed to the idea of God having that effect on people, but I still remained somewhat guarded.

After the video, the faculty prayed for us, and suddenly our school turned upside down. Hard-hearted students were on the ground crying and shaking. Teenagers everywhere were on their knees passionately repenting. When it was time to go to class, they had a hard time getting everyone to leave. I gladly watched as students tried to move but were detained by the Holy Spirit. Some were lying in the hallways under the glory of God. Those of us who could walk had to step over them to go to class.

This phenomenon reoccurred throughout the school year. I can remember teens spontaneously prophesying in the stairwell and students praying for one another.

I loved seeing my friends experience God, but I felt nothing different. Though I took part in worship and absorbed every word preached, my tendency to analyze everything hampered my personal experience.

Feeling like an outsider, I became a little envious. Don't get me wrong; I was ecstatic for everyone else and confident God and I were friends. I just couldn't understand why He left me hanging. Why does God choose one person over another?

I saw the popular girl, who seemed to have everything, sing, prophesy, and cry under God's power. I saw the school's black sheep on the ground unable to get up because of the weight of God's glory. I saw another boy, who was in an ungodly relationship, stuck on the hallway floor repenting. What was wrong with me? I was an obedient Christian, leader in my youth group, lover of God, and on the worship team. Why could I only *see* God move but not *feel* Him?

The Solution

Within our design is a nagging desire for something more. The purpose of this insatiable longing is to draw us closer to God. For my entire life I've had this deep desire, but my prayer life didn't seem to satisfy.

Restless and discouraged, I longed for more of Him and (if I'm being honest) also more of the world. It has taken years to figure out how to be fully, completely, and overly satisfied with the presence of God day in and day out.

Yes, the next level of God's presence is attainable! I want to help people discover the depths and the heights they can reach in their quiet times with God. Your prayer closet can transform into Heaven's secret place. It's possible to experience a level of intimacy with God which becomes so rich you'll feel His tangible love follow you everywhere you go. Imagine spending each day being head over heels in love. There won't be room to harbor emotional pain or trauma, because you will be so full of His peace and joy. Believe me. Everything pales in comparison to a close relationship with Jesus.

Keeping Busy

Often we get lost in the tasks of the day, as we fill our schedule with activity. When we get still, the unrest in our hearts leaves us feeling a little off. It's like an emptiness we can't shake. As a stay-at-home mom, I've definitely been restless in my home. In the past, when a restless sensation of being late or forgetting something came on me, I assigned myself new tasks to ease the discomfort. Now I know it's the Holy Spirit warning me I need to slow down and address a spiritual issue. As I become aware of my soul's cluttered condition, I ask God to show me the issues He wants to address within my heart.

The desire to keep ourselves busy or entertained is our alarm going off. We can feel it when our love tank (for the Father) is on empty. But as we come to God with no agendas, He will take off a layer of stress. Each encounter will remove a layer. It may be a layer of depression, a layer of anxiety, a layer of trauma, or a layer of wounds. Only our loving Savior can peel away these layers which cause such restlessness.

Have you settled into an accepted level of stress and emotional pain? Keep reading this book and I'll give you the answers I spent years searching for. I'll show you the keys to shedding the ADHD prayer life and teach you to walk in His peace and joy 24/7. No matter how long you've been a Christian, I believe I have some important things God told me to tell you. I can say confidently you will feel challenged and encouraged to press in deeper to God.

So many Christians are missing out. We can't see the endless reserves of peace and joy that are available. It's so painful for God to watch Christians walking around with anxiety and offense, when the solution is so very simple. My prayer is that in the pages of this book you discover the rivers of peace and the fountains of joy which burst from your inner being when you open yourself up to the Father in Heaven.

Turn Up the Frequency

One day I was at my piano singing and crying out to God. I asked Him, "How can I hear You more?" Without a thought, I began singing the phrase, "Turn up the frequency," repeatedly. I stopped singing and wondered, *Why am I singing that? Come on, Shanna, stay focused on God!*

That's when I realized God was trying to tell me something. He was answering my question! How can I hear Him? I needed to turn up the frequency.

This statement has different meanings. First, like any radio signal we have to tune in to the frequency of the channel we're looking for. God's radio station is continuously broadcasting because Heaven never stops. There's music, singing, news, and enlightening words. Plus the DJ is God himself, and there's always a live feed. It's exactly what we need to hear when we need to hear it. The only catch is we must use the right frequency.

Secondly, He was telling me to be consistent at seeking Him daily. Then it will become easier to tune in to God's frequency like tuning in to a radio station. In short, we've got to frequently seek God to tune in to His frequency.

Tune in to His Frequency

The key I was missing in my life was knowing how to receive His frequency. Though I was a faithful Christian, I was not turning off my analytical brain and being vulnerable with my heart. It takes a measure of humility to allow God to come in and see the good, the bad, and the ugly going on in our hearts. To tune in to God, I didn't need to learn what to *do*. Instead, I needed to learn to *be*... be in love, be myself, be cherished, be transformed, be still.

Intensify Your Transmission

> *Teacher which commandment in the law is the greatest?" Jesus answered him, "Love the Lord your God with every passion of your heart, with all the energy of your being, and with every thought that is within you.*
> *(MATTHEW 22:36-37 TPT)*

Your "heart" is your radio receiver and "love" is how you dial into God. Long, tedious prayers don't impress God, but a heart fully after Him will grab His attention.

The transmissions of our hearts intensify when we practice. We can give off signals like hunger, adoration, longing, celebration, joy, and gratitude. These raw passions attract God.

What's more astounding is our heart's broadcast can stretch beyond this world to the very throne of God. Get still and allow your inner being to pour out to Him. You may not physically hear a thing, but a passionate heart will loudly burst through any barrier.

Carried Away by Desire

> *Then suddenly my longings transported me. My divine desires brought me next to my beloved Prince, sitting with Him in His royal chariot. We were lifted together!*
> *(SONG OF SOLOMON 6:12 TPT)*

Worship, carried with our heart's desire, seats us next to God. This verse goes beyond communication with God and points to a special closeness. (Who wouldn't want a flying chariot ride?) It's our feelings, not thoughts, that bring us to God. If we are not feeling it, then neither is God.

Many people expect prayer to be boring, but it shouldn't be. Yes, God is invisible and silent to us in the natural, and trying to have a meaningful relationship with someone who never shows His face or speaks an audible word is mind-numbing. But I've got some excellent news. Right now, God is speaking and revealing Himself to us. We only need to switch on our love to be close enough to hear Him.

> *Blessed is the man whose strength is in thee; In whose heart are the highways to Zion.*
> *(PSALMS 84:5 ASV)*

Why are the highways in our hearts and not our minds? The heart is where we build intimacy. Jesus told us He is a rock people will stumble over. This means His actions will logically trip us up if we try to analyze it with our limited minds.

God enjoys confounding the wise. Just check out the outrageous stuff in the Bible—Moses hits a rock to get water, Elisha told a widow to give her last meal away to have more, and God forsook Jesus on the cross to defeat the power of death and Hell. These testimonies are all illogical.

There's a time for analyzing and studying why God does things, and a time for our minds to relinquish the driver's seat to the heart. This is when we tune in to God. This is when the supernatural takes place. This is when the veil separating Heaven and Earth is lifted.

Receiving His Transmissions

It thrills the Father when we use our hearts to receive His love. For many it's difficult to believe God's love is unconditional. This doubt creates a barrier between us and God. Have you ever tried to have a close relationship with someone who didn't accept your love? It's impossible. You'd have to earn their trust and love first. God has already earned our trust and love, and it's written in the Word of God. We need to get this truth firmly planted into our hearts to better accept His love.

There's this thing I do with my kids when I want to tell them I love them. I say, "You don't even know."

They understand I'm telling them they can't imagine the amount of love I have for them.

They will reply, "Yes, I do, cause you tell me all the time." Then I'll playfully argue, "You may think you know how much I love you, but you're not even close to knowing." This is a picture of the Father's love for us. When we get closer to fathoming His love for us, we are still nowhere near knowing its full depth and height.

How do we tune in to His frequency? The key is to place our focus on love. He wants to show us how valuable and cherished we are, but too often we are squirmy and won't hold still. Getting silent before God allows Him room to speak to our hearts without distraction.

When tuning in to God, shed off any purpose, agenda, or distraction you might have and allow yourself to be honest with how much you need and love Him. Though it may tempt you, resist any urge to whisper a prayer or speak in tongues. Your heart's messages will come across louder than words ever could.

Something happens when we approach God solely to be with Him. The experience becomes less of a business meeting and more of an affectionate encounter. No agendas allowed. All worries, needs, and prayer requests can wait until another time. Instead we should simply rest in the warmth of His love, which can only be felt with our hearts. Each time we stop, wait, and rest, He pulls us closer and closer to His heart.

*Rivers of pain and persecution
will never extinguish this flame.
Endless floods will be unable
to quench this raging fire that
burns within you. Everything
will be consumed. It will stop at
nothing as you yield everything
to this furious fire until it won't
even seem to you like a sacrifice
anymore.*

(SONG OF SOLOMON 8:7 TPT)

Listen for Love

You are training your heart to pick up on our Savior's frequency when you get still and delight in Him. He's telling you He loves you right now! It's a repeating message He will forever broadcast. Can you hear it? His mighty love won't be silenced by your imperfections and failings. According to Song of Songs, His love never stops and will never extinguish. It's a raging fire that will burn until it consumes all. If endless floods can't stop His love, then having a nasty attitude on the freeway won't phase it either. Even now He is burning for you to be near Him.

With practice, His signal will become so strong to your heart that it won't matter what time of day or night it is. You will feel lavished by His love constantly. I must warn you though, you may break out in laughter or tears of joy at inopportune times of the day when He surprises you with more of His frequency. But who cares about people's opinions when you're walking in complete love!

Second Conference

Remember the large prayer line, where everyone fell in the Spirit except for my husband and I? The next year, at the same conference, there was another prayer line. When the minister walked by to pray for me, the power of God smacked me before he reached me. That's the only time I've ever gone completely out. I woke up feeling on top of the world but was actually on top of a bunch of people!

My husband told me an unseen force had thrown me back a few feet, and simultaneously, several people behind me collapsed. There I was, sorry but not sorry I was squishing a bunch of strangers. I had spent that previous year tuning in to love frequently. Every day as I dialed into God's love, I fine-tuned my heart's ability to receive Him. So, when the anointed minister came near me, my spirit picked up on God's frequency loud and clear.

I suspect I had struggled all those years, so I could help others find Him too. If you've been in a dry place with God, it's not because He's forgotten you. Often the largest rewards are waiting for those who have the toughest journey.

The Next Chapters

Now tuning in to God is easy for me. Through my bumpy journey, the discovery of God's love brought me to my most treasured revelation. Now I realize I was sensing Him the whole time, but I wasn't picking up the signals. Once I understood how to get my spiritual foot in the door, the next chapter of my life took off.

Hopefully, you've decided settling for miniscule amounts of His presence won't be your story. The next chapters in this book will unveil what is possible once we learn to tune in to His frequency. I'm talking about healing, hearing, Heaven, and everything in between.

Homework

For the length of one worship song, I encourage you to practice loving God while being perfectly still. (Ok, you're allowed to scratch any itchy spots, but don't go overboard!) Find a place where you're comfortable and without distracting devices or people. God may speak to you or not, but that's not the reason to be still. This challenge is to develop your spiritual radio (so to speak) by focusing on your heart's ability to give and receive love.

Here's a tip. Quietly imagine yourself pouring your love out to the Father and believe (really stretch your faith) that He is pouring His love out on you. The goal is just to love and be loved. Don't think about hearing His voice or feeling His presence.

There are two reasons you shouldn't expect God to speak in this exercise. One is because you will have an *agenda* which can distract from the act of giving and receiving love. Another reason is because listening for God's voice may require you to use your *mind* instead of your heart. You can listen for His voice after this exercise. But for now, practice giving and receiving the frequency of Heaven, love.

-‑ᴜᴫᴫᴫ‑

CHAPTER 2

Establishing Your Rhythm

Every morning when Aaron maintains the lamps, he must burn fragrant incense on the altar. And each evening when he lights the lamps, he must again burn incense in the Lord's presence. This must be done from generation to generation.
(EXODUS 30:7-8 NLT)

T urn up the frequency! God wants us to be more frequent in seeking Him. Most people have a regular morning routine. For me, it includes coffee and snuggling with my little son on the couch before I open my Bible app. Aaron's mornings looked a smidge different. He and his sons were priests following divine directions every morning and evening. As we closely examine the priests' routine, their tasks reveal deep truths. If applied, these truths will catapult us into a deeper relationship with our Heavenly Father.

The Priests

The Bible tells us Jesus is the High Priest, and *as believers we are priests* in His priesthood. In 1 Peter 2:5 it reads, *"Ye also, as living stones, are built up a spiritual house, to be a holy priesthood, to offer up spiritual sacrifices, acceptable to God through Jesus Christ"* (ASV).

As priests, we have responsibilities, and we should know what they are. In Exodus 30 we read that every morning and evening Aaron and his sons had to burn sacrifices, maintain the lamps, and burn incense in the Holy Place, along with many other duties. I'm sure after a while it became second nature as they developed a cadence. To Jehovah, this frequent ritual was a pleasing rhythm. What is your daily rhythm? Does it please God?

Burnt Sacrifices (Praise)

For the priests, the first stop in the outer court of the Tabernacle was the brazen (brass) altar designated for animal sacrifices. A large grill was fitted on top with burning coals underneath. The fire was to never go out once the priest ignited it, but on rare occasions God lit the coals with fire from Heaven (1 Chronicles 21:26 and 2 Chronicles 7:1).

At the Brazen Altar the priest conducted animal, grain, and drink offerings on behalf of the people's sins. These sacrifices were considered acts of praise and worship where the people thanked God for His mercy. It was a sweet aroma to the Lord, because it meant the priests and people were faithfully celebrating the forgiveness of God and keeping their end of the covenant.

Like the priest, we should faithfully bring a sacrifice of praise. What a wonderful way to kickstart our day! And what a wonderful way to welcome the presence of God! When we turn our attention towards Him with thanksgiving and praise, we are aligning our hearts with the frequency of Heaven. It's like calibrating our attitude as we join with the continuous praises resounding in Heaven.

The Coal of Fire (Jesus' Sacrifice)

A coal from the Brazen Altar symbolizes the purification of Jesus' sacrifice. The priests chose a fresh coal from the Altar and brought it into the Holy Place. They lit the Lampstand and the incense only with a coal burning with pure, holy fire. Today we don't need a hot coal to get our prayer life started, because Jesus' death and resurrection was enough to purify us from our sins. When we obtain it, we are lit up with His light. Don't worry; being *lit* is a good thing when you're talking about the things of God.

We can be ignited by the holy fire of Jesus. When we accept His sacrifice as purification for our sins, He starts a fire in our souls. The requirements of the priests are shadows of how we can receive holy fire from the sacrifice of the Spotless Lamb. Jesus is the coal that will burn our impurities up, giving us a clean slate.

Now we have a fiery coal from the altar, but we can't stop there. Let's ask God to set us on fire. His holy fire consecrates us for His divine purposes.

Daily asking for God's forgiveness and fire doesn't frustrate Him. He enjoys it when we consistently seek Him. Make it a top priority to have a frequent quiet-time. The faithfulness of our prayer life will strengthen our connection with Him and cause our hearts to be refined by fire.

The Oil (Holy Spirit)

The oil the priest poured into the lamp kept the flame burning. Before you go out and buy a lifetime supply of essential oils, know the oil I'm talking about is spiritual. *Oil is symbolic for the Holy Spirit and His anointing.* The wick is dry without oil, and so are we without the Holy Spirit.

Likewise, our spirits are the lamps. We need oil throughout our day to feed the fire ignited in us. When Jesus sets us on fire, we start off hot. Being on fire for God will quickly dwindle, unless we fill up with the oil of the Holy Spirit. To skip the oil is the same as asking for forgiveness and then stopping there. God not only takes our sins, but He give us His Spirit to help us keep the fire blazing. It's a give and take situation, where we win both ways.

Acts 2:4 says, "*And they were all filled with the Holy Spirit and began to speak with other tongues, as the Spirit gave them utterance*" (ASV). Usually when people encountered the Holy Spirit, the Bible described them as being "*filled*". Like lamps, we need a filling of oil. If the Spirit of God hasn't poured into you His power with the evidence of speaking in tongues, then I urge you to ask Him for this vital gift. Faithfully receive oil for your lamp, so your fire won't burn out during the day. A violent gust of life's problems could surprise you at any moment. *Praying in the Holy Spirit is an enormous part of a Christian's defense strategy.* This isn't something you can ignore.

The Wick (Us)

We are the wick. I once saw a demonstration of how the priest trimmed the lamp's wick. I learned you can't have too much wick protruding out from the lamp or it will blaze too brightly, use up the oil, and burn through the wick too quickly. After generations of trial and error, the priest knew the optimal length for the wick. Let's be like an oil-saturated wick, so we won't step too far out of the presence and power of God.

When I become a prideful person, who is relying on my own strength, it is just like the wick venturing too far out of the oil. Stepping out in my own ability might seem to be an efficient idea at first. This bypasses all that pesky time asking God questions and even more time waiting for answers. And what if God says no? How inconvenient!

Pride misleads us to lean on our own skills and abilities. In our impatience we will see faster results under our control, but it won't lead to good results. Using our own strength would cause burn out. At the start, we may seem like a gleaming blaze of fire, but eventually we'd have nothing but darkness. However, when we are hidden in the *oil*, we will be a light to others. We will learn to use less of our own strength and rely more on Christ's power.

We get our "essential oil" by speaking in tongues. And boy, is it essential! When the Holy Spirit is on us, we have peace, joy, energy, wisdom, healing and so much more. There are essential oils on the market for all those things, but not as effective. I want the original! When speaking in tongues becomes a routine in our lives, our flame is enduring and our light is bright.

Burn Incense (Prayer)

As the priest continued in their morning rhythm, they came to the Altar of Incense. Again, they used the coal from the Brazen Altar to light the incense. They prayed and worshipped as the perfumed aroma lifted up in ribbons of smoke. Every morning and evening they repeated this ritual to please God.

Today we don't need incense to appease God in prayer. Like the coal, Jesus has lit us with His holy fire, so *our prayers are now fragrant incense* with the authority of Jesus. Our petitions carry a new level of power, because we have been purified with Jesus.

> *And the smoke and fragrant aroma of the incense, with the prayers of the saints (God's people), ascended before God from the angels' hand.*
> *(REVELATIONS 8:4 AMP)*

God doesn't just hear our prayers; He smells and sees our prayers too! Faithfully praying to God every morning and evening was a requirement for the priests, but for us it's an opportunity. An opportunity to thrill God with perfumed prayer and worship. He is moved by our prayers because they carry the purity, authority, and fire of Jesus. Each time we come to God in prayer, our faithfulness establishes His hand on our lives, and His favor covers us throughout the day.

The Rhythm of Faithfulness

Faithfulness is being repetitively consistent in what God requires us to do. Like the priests who remained steadfast, it's vital we learn the discipline of daily praising, repenting, and praying. How I meet with God, might look different for you. Whether we pray in the morning or evening is not important. It's the consistency of keeping a quiet time that will draw the presence of the Lord.

Think of it this way. The Bible tells us a thousand years is like a day to God. We may imagine our daily prayers as becoming monotonous to God, but to Him it goes by faster. Over the years our consistent prayer times sound more like a rhythmic beat. Faithfulness becomes the tempo to our life's song. This persistent pursuit draws the heart of the Father. And like a catchy tune, your faithfulness brings Him great pleasure.

God seems to love repetition. It's displayed in the timely rising and setting of the sun. We can experience it in the constant ever-changing of the seasons. He designed the world we see around us with patterns, mathematics, logic, and reason. When He spoke the universe into existence, He only needed to speak once to set it in the perpetual motion still moving today.

When the priests repeatedly honored God in the first and last part of the day, it overjoyed Him. The thing which pleased His heart wasn't only the lit lamp or the burning incense, but the faithfulness.

Their daily rhythm was a savory act of worship to the Lord.

Faithfulness is His Dwelling Place

I will declare that Your love stands firm forever, that You have established Your faithfulness in Heaven itself.
(PSALMS 89:2 NIV)

God is faithful. All of creation hold facets of His faithful nature. There's faithfulness in the sky, which is the Earth's atmosphere encompassing the rhythmic seasons and weather patterns. We also see faithfulness in space, where cosmic bodies display the reliable movements of laws and physics.

The Father established faithfulness in Heaven too, which is the place of His throne and the home of many saints and angels. Heaven operates in God's perfect order. He is the rhythm and the rhyme. He is the rising and the setting of the sun. He is the Alpha and Omega. Just as a song improves with a solid tempo, so the Lord's rhythm improves our lives when we frequently seek Him. So, if we want to encounter Heaven, we should prioritize faithfulness.

In Psalms 89:8 it reads, "*Who is like You, Lord God Almighty? You, Lord, are mighty, and Your faithfulness surrounds You*" (NIV). Wait a minute! Why does faithfulness surround God? Let's examine this.

If God surrounds Himself with faithfulness, that means He resides in faithfulness. It *is* His dwelling place. So, by being faithful, we are aligned with His presence.

The original Hebrew word used here for *"surrounds"* is *"sebibah."* It means the environment around something or someone, the territory encircling. Another definition for this word is *"circuits,"* which suggest the motion of a pattern, like the circuits of the sea's currents. When I hear this, I picture order going out and coming in His presence. He speaks and the directives of His plan go forth and return to Him having accomplished His purpose. We can see this mentioned in Isaiah 55:11 when God said, *"So shall my word be that goes forth from my mouth; It will not return to me void, But it shall accomplish what I please, And it shall prosper in the thing for which I sent it"* (NKJV).

In Psalms 89:14 David goes a step further and says, *"... love and faithfulness go before You"* (NIV). This shows us when He arrives somewhere, faithfulness is established there first. Like a red carpet laid out before royalty, faithfulness welcomes the King of kings. Allow God to establish faithfulness in you. He's telling us, "If you want more of Me, then turn up your frequency." Think of faithfulness as the stones used to build the dwelling placed for the King. We must stay consistent because each quiet time welcomes in more of the Almighty.

Notice how the verse mentions that "love" also goes before God. In the previous chapter, we discussed how love is the secret to tuning in to God. If we pair love with faithfulness, then we are stumbling upon a key revelation King David understood. The favor of God in David's life is a testament to the importance of having both love and faithfulness.

How can we increase our love? As we seek to know Him in the Word and in prayer, He becomes irresistible. Our love grows with each new revelation we acquire. And when we understand He is not just a historical figure long gone, but a living God who is easily accessible, we love Him all the more.

Reasons to be Faithful

How valuable it is to visit with God and fill our lamp with oil. A faithful prayer life will align us with the rhythm of the Father's heartbeat. Like adjusting the antennas on a radio, we're positioning ourselves to stay connected to Him.

Imagine hearing His voice before making an important decision or feeling His peace when everyone around is arguing. This is the life He wants us to lead, but only the faithful will see its full reward on Earth. If we're wanting to tune in to Heaven, then establishing faithfulness in prayer and obedience is a must. Besides, God is pleased when we're faithful! Do we truly need another reason?

Homework

Answer these questions.

1. *Am I consistent in reading the Bible?*

2. *Am I consistent in repenting and allowing the Holy Spirit to correct me?*

3. *Am I consistent in praying (especially in tongues) daily?*

4. *Without making myself overwhelmed, what can I improve to be more frequent with God?*

By asking these questions you are allowing God to shed light on the true condition of your faithfulness. It's easy to ignore problems, but this is one issue that should not be overlooked. Be sensitive to the conviction of the Holy Spirit when deciding what changes to make. And don't make your consistency become dogmatic, because it will only lead to shame and failure. Instead let your faithfulness be an act of love, and your rhythm be an act of worship.

CHAPTER 3

Your Receiver

H ave you seen the part in *Sister Act* where Whoopi Goldberg helped the timid nun sing by pressing on her diaphragm? This shy, little nun shifted from her head voice to her chest voice, as soon as she learned from where to sing. Astonished at the volume, her sound resonated throughout the air. She had tapped into the hidden potential she always possessed. So, in this chapter you're the nun and I'm Whoopi. And I'm about to help you find where you hold the power.

Guarded Heart

If God is a DJ broadcasting from Heaven, then our hearts are the radio receivers. We tune in to Heaven's frequency when our hearts are dialed in to love. God's signals come as visions, dreams, discernments, divine glory, holy fire, and any other way He can connect with us.

All those years I couldn't feel God was the result of a heart problem. Unfortunately, my receiver wasn't picking up on His messages. To find these encounters, I didn't know to focus on my love and desire for Him. Instead, I exhausted myself trying to figure out how to convince Him to draw close. It was difficult for me to trust that His love was unconditional. I reined in my affection because subconsciously I feared His rejection.

Some people don't need an explanation on how to love God, because they already have unguarded hearts. Sadly, I needed it explained with a power point presentation and visual aids. I was clueless to the fact I had guarded my heart. Somewhere in my childhood I learned feelings were bad, crying was a sign of weakness, and being mushy with love was unwanted. Because of this misconception, I had unknowingly built walls, which hindered my relationship with God.

My spiritual radio needed to be free and clear to receive from Heaven, but how could I change if I didn't know I needed help? It's not like I've experienced extreme trauma and abuse. Eventually, the Lord showed me the little hurts and fears in my life dampened my ability to hear Him. Over the years, He gave me a series of revelations which have helped me heal and stay healed. In this chapter and the next, I want to show you this inner-healing process He revealed to me.

The first step to repairing my heart was locating it. It never occurred to me that knowing *where* my heart was would set me on the path to freedom, but it did. So, let's begin by finding your receiver, because you can't adjust the dial if you can't find the radio.

Where's the Heart?

The Bible mentions the "heart" around 900 times (depending on the version). With all this talk about our hearts, it is clear God is saying the heart is important. Go ahead and point to your heart right now. If you pointed to your chest then good job, you paid attention in school. However, the Old Testament Hebrews might have disagreed with you. They considered the gut as the spiritual center of man. They believed our emotions and heart were in the inward parts of the belly.

The word "heart" in many of the New Testament verses is translated from *Kardiais*. This refers more to the center of a person and the source of their emotions. It rarely means the blood-pumping organ. Colossians 3:12 says, "*Put on therefore, as the elect of God, holy and beloved, **bowels** of mercies, kindness, humbleness of mind, meekness, and long-suffering*" (KJV). In this verse newer Bible translations use the term "heart" instead of "bowels."

The Greek word for "heart" is *splagehnon* (try to pronounce that correctly). They often used this term for "spleen" and can also mean strength, intestines, pity, sympathy, bowels, inwards affection, and tender mercies. There are many verses and definitions which portray the heart as our gut, but I will spare you.

Throughout the day our gut responds to the array of our emotions. What happens to us physically when we find something hilarious? Our stomachs convulse and cause us to giggle, scream, or snort. In extreme cases of laughter, we find ourselves unable to breathe with tears in our eyes. At this point our stomachs have locked down and rendered us incapable of explaining what is so funny to any onlookers. When we cry something similar takes place. Our stomach will moan or shake as we weep from our hearts.

There are other emotions which influence our belly. What happens when we are nervous? Our digestive tract lets us know it doesn't want any food, and sometimes it even kicks food out. How about depression, stress, fear, love, or excitement? Every one of these feelings affects the stomach. No wonder the Jews saw our belly as the seat of our emotions and the place where our heart is. So now that you know, you may want to put a spleen on your next Valentine card. Just saying... it's Biblical.

We cry, laugh, shout, scream, and moan from our gut and emotions. The same goes with singing. Have you heard the advice to sing from your heart? You can tell the difference between a singer going through the motions and a singer using their raw emotions. The second is so much better.

God designed our voices perfectly. At the top end is our noise maker (mouth), and at the other end is our diaphragm (heart area) and lungs (spirit area). The term "Spirit" comes from the Latin word *spiritus* meaning breath. Our spirit and emotions are where an affective song originates, and when it's breathed out something amazing happens. The song's message touches the heart of the listener.

Worship's primary purpose is to move God's heart. If you're a singer or a musician, then learn to worship God from your emotions. I've heard people argue loud music in church just gives the crowd an emotional experience, and it's not true worship. I respectfully disagree, because worship is empty unless it's filled with love—an emotion. How can we thank Him, praise Him, celebrate Him, and long for Him without emotions? And what is a powerful tool we can use to stir emotions? Music.

In Spirit and in Truth

You may be thinking, *But all this emotional stuff can be dangerous, because the Bible tell us the heart is deceitful.* You're right. We can't trust our hearts, but we can trust the Holy Spirit and the Word. The Holy Spirit inside us directs our hearts (2 Thessalonians 3:5). When we depend on Him, He teaches us how to pray and how to worship.

We should fill our souls with the Word of God. What we ingest we will sing out. The more we learn who God is in the Bible, the more reasons we have to worship Him. The scriptures are the logs, and the Holy Spirit is the fire. When you put them together, you've got roasted marshmallows of worship. Maybe that's not a thing, but you get my point.

One of my favorite stories in the Bible is when Jesus spoke to the woman at the well in John 4. As they were chit-chatting back and forth, you can tell she was getting closer to her big concern. *"'Sir,' the woman said, 'I can see that you are a prophet. Our ancestors worshiped on this mountain, but you Jews claim that the place where we must worship is in Jerusalem'"* (John 4:19-20 NIV). She wanted to know the correct way to worship God. She was a half-Jew who was required to hike a particular mountain to worship while the full-blooded Jews journeyed to Jerusalem. During those days, people had to travel to a designated spot if they wanted to worship God.

Jesus told her she didn't have to go anywhere. He said, *"Yet a time is coming and has now come when the true worshipers will worship the **Father** in the **Spirit** and in **truth**, for they are the kind of worshipers the Father seeks"* (verse 23). Jesus explained that the Father is seeking worshipers who are filled with the Holy Spirit and the Word of God.

Right now, the Father is searching for the true worshipers. Will He find your heart tuned in to the Holy Spirit? Will He find your heart full of the truth of the Word?

Where is the Holy Spirit?

Because you are his sons, God sent the Spirit of his Son into our hearts, the Spirit who calls out, "Abba, Father."
(GALATIANS 4:6 NIV)

Have you ever heard truth and something inside of you burned in agreement? That's the fire of the Holy Spirit burning in your inner man. You can call it your heart, innermost being, depths, or gut. The Bible specifies the Holy Spirit is in our hearts. "... *He anointed us, set his seal of ownership on us, and put his Spirit in our hearts as a deposit, guaranteeing what is to come*" (2 Corinthians 1:22 NIV).

When I was a children's pastor, I saw many children get filled with the Holy Spirit and speak in tongues. They would say they felt fire or a weird feeling in their stomach. Children don't always have the ability to put how they feel into words. A few said they felt like throwing up. I knew they weren't nauseous because they were smiling and celebrating. I think they were trying to articulate they felt the urge to release the flow of the Spirit of God from their bellies.

So far, we determined our spiritual hearts are in our abdomens, and now we're discovering the Holy Spirit is in our hearts (Romans 5:5) (2 Galatians 4:6). Why is this important to know? Because if we want to move in His power, then we need to know where the power source is.

> *He that believeth on me, as the*
> *scripture hath said, out of his belly*
> *shall flow rivers of living water.*
> *(JOHN 7:38 KJV)*

To connect with God, I find it helps to drop my focus down to the Holy Spirit in my inner being. I do this when I want to feel His presence, hear Him, or pray over people. Sometimes I place my hand on my stomach to remind myself this is where the God of the universe lives. And by faith I draw from His love and power.

Spend some time in worship with your hand on your belly. Can you feel anything? It helps me when I imagine love flowing out of me like a river towards God. Don't be discouraged if you feel nothing at first. I had to practice before it became easy. Now when I remain on the emotion of love, it takes a few seconds before I can sense something shift. It's as if the Lord changes the atmosphere in and around me.

Power-Packed

The Holy Spirit is the battery which powers our radio receivers. As the Spirit abounds in us, the voice of God becomes amplified. With practice your heart will learn to receive more and more from God. You just have to quiet your surroundings and acknowledge the presence of God living in you. He gave us a powerful tip when He said, *"Be still and know that I am God"* (Psalms 46:10a ASV).

Water, fire, wind, light, and oil have always been symbolic for the Holy Spirit. These elements have something in common, they have no solid shape. The Spirit of God flows and moves. He is the power behind every work of God. Interestingly, in the natural, man has learned to use these same substances (water, fire, wind, light, and oil) and convert them to energy.

The Holy Spirit was there at creation, empowering the Word spoken by the Father. If you think tsunamis or hurricanes are powerful, then you haven't seen anything yet. In fact, the intensity of the sun combined with the 100 billion other stars in the cosmos are just the fringes of what the Spirit can do (Job 26:14). Jesus tells us we will do greater works than Him, when we receive the Holy Spirit (John 14:12-17). If Jesus created the universe with only His voice, and He said we can do the same plus more, then there must be a lot of potential energy living inside us!

The power of the entire universe lives in us! Yet we barely use it. That's why it's important to keep seeking God and building a relationship with Him. He wants to demonstrate power and authority through us, but He needs us to put Him first.

It's vital we wait, listen, and be still in His presence. Isaiah 40:31 says, *"But they that wait upon the Lord shall renew their strength; they shall mount up with wings as eagles; they shall run, and not be weary; and they shall walk, and not faint*" (KJV). How do we get strength? We wait. If you're not taking the time each day to be still with the Holy Spirit, then you are missing out on that boost of power needed for the day. And it's not just you who is missing out, but those around you too.

Word Power

The same force behind the words "*Let there be light*" can empower your words. Most people don't realize there's power in what they say. Spirit-filled Christians must be careful with their tongues. That thing is a weapon which can heal or kill, because God's anointing is on it. If you've said anything negative over yourself, over others, or over a situation, repent and break it in Jesus' name. When you speak negative words, you are cursing situations and people. Guard that tongue! God wants us to bless with our mouths. Our words are so powerful the Bible tells us we can move mountains with them when we have faith.

> *And I will give you the keys of the kingdom of Heaven, and whatever you bind on earth will be bound in Heaven, and whatever you loose on earth will be loosed in Heaven.*
> *(MATTHEW 16:19 NIV)*

These are the bona fide, authentic, actual **keys of Heaven**. With them, you can bind and loose things with your spoken words. He's given you the power! At any time, you are able to bind life to your health, relationships, ministry, or finances. Furthermore, you can loose any curse, enemy, or effect of sin from your life, and it's a done deal! It's almost as if God is saying to us, we can ask anything and it will be done. Oh wait, He is saying that! "*You may ask me for anything in my name, and I will do it*" (John 14:13 NIV).

Praise with Power

If "all power" infuses our words, does that mean our singing can be powerful too? Yes! When we sing from our gut and tap into the Holy Spirit's power, we go from singing a cute tune to dismantling the armies of Hell. It's time to release that river flowing from your belly. Your melody is your weapon.

You won't defeat the enemy with only positive thoughts. You've got to use sound. The Bible doesn't say we overcome by the *consideration* of our testimony, but by the *words* of our testimony (Revelations 12:11). When we praise, we are testifying against the demonic and weakening them to their demise.

If we could see what goes on in the spirit realm, we could see the battle raging above us between demons and angels. Our shouts of praise could look like supersonic blasts impairing the enemy enough for the angels to run them through with their swords. Who knows? But one thing is for sure, our words of praise pack a mean punch.

When I worship before the Lord, I want every note to carry the anointing of the Holy Spirit. I focus in on my deep love for God and sense Him in my gut. It will do no good to sing without His power. I'm wasting my breath if He's not breathing through me. When I allow myself to bask in how much He loves me, how I love Him, and how He loves others, I'm tapping into His frequency. I'm tuning in to His radio channel. With practice it becomes easier and clearer.

The Receiver

Now, do you know where your heart is? It is your personal portal to God. Any time, day or night, you can reach Him when you drop your focus down to your heart. Like the nun in *Sister Act* all the power of the Holy Spirit is within you waiting to be tapped into. You can now have a powerful voice (no promises that it will sound as good as the nun's).

Our hearts have the resources of revelation, healing, and breakthrough just sitting there ready to be accessed. It's a game changer when we realize how God equips us. This knowledge has transformed my life drastically, and I can't wait to tell you how finding my heart led to freeing my heart. Keep reading, because this is only the tip of the iceberg.

Homework

Put on some worship music. Place your hand on your stomach and sing from your heart. Hold nothing back!

By doing this you will be worshiping in spirit and in truth. This will increase your heart's ability to allow the Holy Spirit to empower your worship. And with practice, you'll find He will direct you into some adlibbing or even a new song. Singing from your deep passions will train your heart/receiver to tune in to Heaven's frequency.

CHAPTER 4

Soaking Waves

In 2012, I was at home with my two boys flipping through TV channels, and I stopped on *The 700 Club*. Suddenly, waves of the Holy Spirit overcame me. My kids wondered why mom was crying and laughing without warning. I had no idea who or what was on the program, but my curiosity awoke. It was at the end of the show, and a couple was ministering to the studio audience. All I gathered was that these people were carrying an intensity of God's presence that was next level.

Before I knew what hit me, another wave of God's glory captivated me. Using the couch to pull myself off the floor, I decided to investigate further. I wasn't about to miss out on such a large quantity of the Holy Spirit operating in my life.

After some digging, I discovered John and Carol Arnott were the ones ministering to *The 700 Club's* studio audience. They were teaching about "soaking," and the anointing I felt through my television was unbelievable. Revival hit John and Carol's church in Toronto in 1994, and the Holy Spirit still moves mightily in their congregation. Soaking has been instrumental in this revival.

No Agenda

He offers a resting place for me in His luxurious love. His tracks take me to an oasis of peace, the quiet brook of bliss.
(PSALMS 23:2 TPT)

Soaking is resting in God's love with no agenda. It's a time to leave your prayer requests at the door in order to rest in His caring arms. Learning about God doesn't compare to experiencing Him. According to the Bible, He is love, which means He is an emotion. A relationship with Him must be felt. Since the time I started turning up my frequency with soaking, my biggest change is I have fallen more in love with God.

Usually soaking requires a level of silence and stillness we're not used to. We can be like preschoolers who can't hold still for a hug. We tell ourselves, "that's boring," or, "I want to be doing something." Don't worry; He will help us get past our squirminess. At first, it may seem like a mundane chore or even an act of punishment, but once His love washes over us, it is the most exhilarating thing we will ever do.

The word "soaking" is a modern term. This type of prayer has been practiced by many powerful men and women of God for centuries. Miracle-working ministers like Smith Wigglesworth and Kathryn Kuhlman put great emphasis on being still and waiting on God. If you have problems with the word "soaking" then call it whatever you want, just don't knock it until you try it.

How to Soak

Think of it as quality time with your Father. Find a distraction-free zone that's comfortable. Soft worship music is fine, or total silence will work too. Sometimes before I get silent it helps to speak in tongues a bit. In the first moments it takes effort to wait on God. It doesn't help when the enemy reminds you of all the things that need to get done. So, go ahead and write them down. Then put the list aside. This will keep your mind from getting preoccupied by lingering responsibilities.

Once the distractions are gone it's time to fall back into the Father's arms. Imagine you're just sinking into His love. As you focus on the Holy Spirit inside you, He will communicate with you. Your only job is to soak up His love and pay attention to anything He shows you. Let go of your thoughts, so His thoughts can direct you. Also, it's important you don't start praying immediately after He tells you something (I still struggle with this). Zip that lip! He may have more to say.

What Happens

When you soak, you are being recharged by the Holy Spirit. His love will pour all over you and transform you from the inside out. Often, He will reveal how He thinks and feels about you. The closer you get to Him, the more your self-image will become aligned with how He sees you. By offering your undivided attention, you are valuing His heart. God can have anything He wants, yet His greatest desire is intimacy with you.

Soaking in the presence of God is the way to the Father's heart. As we tune in, we're being changed by His glory. Each encounter will refine us, burning away all fear, pride, pain, and lies. His passion transforms us and defines our identity. Like refined gold, we will begin to reflect the one we spend time with, Jesus.

God Values our Closeness

The Father went to substantial lengths to meet with you. You are His child. He longs for your love and is excited to spend time with you. We don't see all the obstacles He overcame to be with us. Think of the millions of ancestors who are in your generational line. We can't know how many times God gave our forefathers mercy.

I'm sure many in my bloodline deserved to be wiped off the face of the Earth. I like to believe God knew I was coming and preserved my family all the way back to Adam. God has given generations of people chance after chance, so you and I could be here right now in His grace. Since creation, God has endured so much for us to come to Him, even though we (humans) don't deserve His mercy.

Why would the Father do so much just so we could be redeemed and allowed into His presence? That kind of love makes little sense to our natural minds. But if we understood how much value the Father places on these small encounters, I suspect we would do everything in our power to soak in the secret place as often as we could.

10 Virgins

> *At that time the kingdom of Heaven will be like ten virgins who took their lamps and went out to meet the bridegroom. Five of them were foolish and five were wise. The foolish ones took their lamps but did not take any oil with them. The wise ones, however, took oil in jars along with their lamps. The bridegroom was a long time in coming, and they all became drowsy and fell asleep. At midnight the cry rang*

*out: "Here's the bridegroom!
Come out to meet him!" then all
the virgins woke up and trimmed
their lamps.*

*The foolish ones said to the wise,
"Give us some of your oil; our
lamps are going out."*

*"No," they replied, "there may
not be enough for both us and
you. Instead, go to those who sell
oil and buy some for yourselves."
But while they were on their way
to buy the oil, the bridegroom
arrived. The virgins who were
ready went in with him to the
wedding banquet. And the door
was shut. Later the others also
came. "Lord, Lord," they said,
"open the door for us!"*

*But he replied, "Truly I tell you; I
don't know you."*
(MATTHEW 25:1-12 NIV)

Jesus told us there were two kinds of virgins who
represent two kinds of people. Those who go to God
for oil and those who don't. In this story oil represents
intimacy with the Holy Spirit. Resting in His pres-

ence supplies the oil which fuels our lamp (spirit) for a while. Eventually we must get more.

I have a good hunch the bridegroom in this story is also the same person who gifted the wise virgins their oil. It makes sense because in the Bible "oil" represents the anointing and intimacy with God. The Bible also tells us Jesus is the "Bridegroom." Considering the symbolism of the oil and the bridegroom, we can interpret the five wise virgins got their oil from intimate meetings with the Him. They had met the bridegroom on countless occasions and were in a close relationship with Him. (Normally this story would be disturbing since the groom had so many brides. But this is a parable of how the church is the bride of Christ, so... you can relax.)

The foolish virgins were trying to *buy* oil (relationship), which was the ticket into the marriage feast. You can't earn your way into Heaven with good works or large ministries. God will say, "I don't know you." You have to know Him as a friend and Father. Ministry without a relationship with Him is fake oil. He's not impressed with big congregations or marvelous deeds. He's not even impressed with your gifts and talents. He just wants you.

Fragrant Oil

Another place in the Bible that mentions oil is Song of Solomon 5:13. The verse speaks of fragrant myrrh dripping from the Bridegroom's lips. In Song of Solomon, a sweet-smelling oil represents the intimacy between love-sick lovers. I imagine the five wise virgins obtained their oil by visiting the Bridegroom (Jesus) in the secret place... often. (I can see their fathers now, "Young lady, where did all this oil of intimacy come from?")

God uses the intensity of falling in love to explain His supernatural love. His love goes beyond any kind of earthly love, but the best way He can describe it is by using lovers as an example. However, the love He is talking about is so pure and holy, romantic love pales in its light.

God wants us to come to Him for oil. The person who spends time in God's secret place will bring the fragrant oil of intimacy everywhere they go. And when the Bridegroom comes for the church, He will know the ones who carry His oil and burn with His fire.

Healing in Soaking

> *He heals the wounds of every shattered heart.*
> *(PSALMS 147:3 TPT)*

In 2015, my wonderful mom and I took a Sid Roth tour of Israel. On our bus there was a couple named Dennis Clark and Dr. Jen Clark, who have a ministry focused on inner healing. I had seen them before on an episode of *Sid Roth's It's Supernatural*, but I didn't fully understand what they did. However, it wasn't until they demonstrated their revelation, I started to grasp it and apply it to my life.

One day our group of around 200 tourists was taking a break under a large pavilion. Sid addressed the crowd and introduced this couple. The Clarks claimed they would show us a way to heal our emotional wounds. Then they asked for a volunteer. To my surprise, someone raised their hand. When this brave soul came up, Dennis instructed him to close his eyes and pray while putting his hand on his belly. Once he felt the Holy Spirit, the Clarks told him, "Ask God to reveal where you need healing. The first person or memory which comes to mind is God's answer."

When the man asked, God's reply came in the next moment. He said a painful memory of his father popped into his mind. Next, he was instructed to feel the emotion attached to that memory. At this point the man was weeping, and I was thinking this better work because they've made a grown man cry in front of hundreds of people on his vacation. Once he allowed himself to feel the emotion, they told him, "Now, place all the pain and unforgiveness in your abdominal area. This is where the Holy Spirit lives inside you, and He will take the hurt from you." In a moment, he moved from sorrow to joy. With an enormous grin the man proclaimed he felt no pain from the memory, and a heavy burden had lifted. Hallelujah!

Goodbye Hurt

Since then, I've put this into practice, and it works! I won't let hurt remain for very long. Usually within an hour of getting offended, I will get still, wait for the presence of God, feel the pain of the moment, and present it to God in my gut (heart). When the offense is difficult to let go, I say, "Holy Spirit, please take it." Without fail, the Holy Spirit has taken every emotional hurt, bitterness, and trauma I've given to Him in a matter of seconds. I'm not kidding!

I want to emphasize the importance of placing the pain in your stomach. This is the key to a quick breakthrough. The Clarks describe it as "dropping down." It sounds strange, but there is no better way to explain it since it's something that is done spiritually instead of physically. It takes a measure of imagination to feel the tension of the memory in my chest and shift it to my gut. When I do this, I'm exposing my wound to the Healer who lives inside me. Every time I'm amazed at how quickly He takes my burden.

I know I'm free when afterwards I recall the memory with no pain present. It's hard to express what it's like to be heavily burdened and instantly as free as a child. Now my hurt feelings wash away as soon as I take time to give them to God. This way God helps me maintain healthy emotions while staying soft-hearted.

Some pain, fears, and traumas have many layers, that's why it's important to ask God to show us a specific event to work on. We shouldn't address every emotion at once. A victim who has survived years of abuse should deal with one incident at a time over the course of a season.

Following the lead of the Holy Spirit is vital, because we can never be completely certain where to start when it comes to dealing with the intricacies of the mind and emotions. Even counselors and psychologist can only use educated guesses. Let the Holy Spirit be your guide, and you'll find you won't be too overwhelmed. You can focus on one pain at a time and trust God knows what He's doing.

Hello Trust

This technique of "dropping down" works because you exercise faith when you place it in His hands. This is different from just crying out to God while wondering if He cares or if things will ever improve. Trusting Him to take it in that moment (not down the road) will change how you deal with pain. This is more effective than feeling alone and sorry for yourself while hoping one day in the future He will ease the torment a little. If you're holding out for an emotional healing, trust He can do it now, even if the world says it takes years to recover.

Being Vulnerable

Remembering and embracing the full weight of our emotions causes us to be *honest* and *vulnerable*. When we're hurt, our natural tendency is to be defensive and cover up how we feel. But we can't cover anything from God. This approach to healing is like unwrapping the bandages on our emotional wounds and holding it out (in our gut) waiting for the Spirit of God to take it.

I've noticed that the times I hold the hurt in my chest it remains. But when I place the hurt lower in my abdomen, there is healing within seconds. It's like I stop grasping it and allow the Holy Spirit, who dwells in my heart, to take it. It feels vulnerable, but God is faithful to take what you give Him every time. If you want to learn more about this subject, then I encourage you to read Dennis and Dr. Jen Clark's books.

Why would the Father give His only Son's life, so imperfect people could come to Him? What is so important about meeting with us? Everything He does points to one goal, *being united with His children.*

I hope by now you are seeing how valuable it is to be still and soak in God's presence. He desires us to experience the restoration power of simply being close to Him. You could build enormous churches or create exquisite music, but if you're not coming to soak in His oil of intimacy, then your efforts are meaningless.

Homework

Healing your Heart is vital to clearly receiving Heaven's frequency. Here's how to do it.

1. *Pray or worship until you are focused on God.*

2. *Ask God to bring up any person or situation where you need healing.*

3. *Feel the emotions attached to the person or event.*

4. *Place the emotions in your gut, where the Holy Spirit is there to take it from you.*

5. *Wait in faith until you sense the burden of the memory slip away.*

6. *Think of the person or situation again and compare your new emotional response to how you used to feel. The negative feelings, such as unforgiveness or hurt, should be less or completely gone.*

7. *Thank God, because you've just been spared years of therapy.*

CHAPTER 5

Hunger Signals

C an you guess the most famous sermon ever preached? I'll give you a hint: it was on a mount (Bible talk for mini-mountain). When Jesus preached the *Sermon on the Mount* (Matthew 5-7), He introduced the most profound teachings ever spoken. The amount of revelation in the first line alone is a lifetime's worth of wisdom. He said, "*Blessed are the poor in spirit, for theirs is the kingdom of Heaven*" (Matthew 5:3 ASV).

When you picture the poor, what images come to mind? Maybe you visualize a hungry child holding an empty plate, a family who has lost everything in a war-torn country, or a weathered old man with no shelter on a mini-mountain. Would you agree an appropriate definition of "poor" is a person who lacks a necessity?

Why does Jesus say, "Blessed are the poor in spirit"? If He said poor in body, we could assume He meant a sick person. Poor in spirit tells us this person needs something spiritual. They are lacking only what God, who is Spirit, can give. But doesn't everyone need God? If that definition of poor is what He meant, it seems like everyone is poor in spirit. Perhaps He meant the evil sinners are the poor in spirit, but then why would God be blessing them? Instead, Jesus was talking about people who recognize their poverty. Every person needs God, but few realize it. A person who understands they can't be righteous on their own, is poor in spirit.

Learning from the Poor

A poor person learns to humble themselves and ask for help. They understand that by themselves they can't survive. Hunger demands priority and affects all of their decisions. Even their worldview is seen through the perspective of hunger.

We can learn a lot from the poor. God wants us to humble ourselves and ask for help. We need to recognize we are starving for Him. Unfortunately, we usually try to silence our hunger with the things of the world, forgetting how desperately we need Him. The world won't satisfy or sustain us. Imagine eating rocks to appease our hunger pangs.

As a US citizen it can be hard understanding how poor in spirit I actually am. We have so much of our physical needs met here, but there is a downside. We've missed out on blessings because we've learned to ignore those hunger pangs. We must allow ourselves time to dwell on how badly we need Him in every area of our lives. When He becomes our everything, that's when we are "poor in Spirit."

He Wants to be Wanted

Hunger draws God's attention. Eagerly, He listens for the irresistible frequency of our desire. It pleases Him and brings Him great joy when His children recognize their need.

Have you ever tried to pursue a deep relationship with someone who didn't want you? Did they turn your friendship into their required duty which they suffered through? That would feel awful. If someone thought that way about me, I'd tell them, "Don't bother yourself, I can make new friends." God wants to be wanted just like we do.

The Bible tells us David was a man after God's own heart. David filled the book of Psalms with his longing and hunger for God. Psalms 27:4 is the perfect picture of David's need for God. I love how *The Passion Translation* depicts David's deep desires. *"Here's the one thing I crave from God, the one thing I seek above all else: I want the privilege of living with Him every moment in His house, finding the sweet loveliness of His face, filled with awe, delighting in His glory and grace. I want to live my life so close to Him He takes pleasure in my every prayer"*. David knew exactly how to bring God joy. He showered God with worship and prayer. He expressed his need and delighted in

God's response. Most importantly, the Almighty looked beyond the poetic words and took pleasure in David's total dependence.

Revelation Spurs Hunger

God can spot a faker. Either we need God, or we don't. But how can we understand how much we need God, if we don't know Him? As we crack open the Bible, our faith is built up. We read about all the feats God accomplished and suddenly the possibilities are endless. For example, when we realize the same God of Moses lives in us, then we can count on God splitting the sea that rages in front of us. According to the Sermon on the Mount, more revelation results in more hunger. And more hunger means more of the Kingdom of Heaven.

If you're not sure if you hunger for God like you should, then ask Him to increase it. Allow Him to show you how poor you really are. It's difficult to see ourselves as poor if we're dressed nice and driving a nice car, but those things can create an illusion. Medication can cover illness, alcohol can cover our inner wounds, entertainment can cover the noise of our convicted conscience, and human approval can cover up our awareness of God's disapproval. Deep down we know relationships will never satisfy in the long-term, fame will eventually be empty, and stuff only brings us temporary joy. It's time to get real with yourself and ask God about the exact state of your spiritual poverty. How hungry are you?

Awakened Hunger

There was a season where I unintentionally blamed God for not bringing revival when I expected it. I didn't realize I was blaming God. I just gradually stopped anticipating and asking for the miraculous. I even told myself it was "spiritual maturity" to not get swept away with imagining what is possible with God. Whenever I prayed, I doubted in the back of my mind. I didn't know it, but I wasn't letting myself fully trust Him because of the previous let downs.

Deep down, I understood hungering after God meant vulnerability. Sometimes God's answer to our prayer is "no," or maybe it's "wait." Either way, I had felt defeated and stopped hoping for a powerful move of God. I became grumpy, and without realizing it, I lost all motivation to dream. I felt like I was striving to keep my head above the waters of the mundane. As a result, I swallowed my emotional disappointments rather than trusting again.

Allowing Myself to Hunger

Recently, my mom and I attended the "Light the Fire Again Conference 2019" in Pensacola, Florida. I was glad for the trip, but didn't allow myself to expect too much. On the second day of the conference there were some young interns praying for people during the lunch break. I asked for prayer from one of the teens who seemed to move in the Holy Spirit. He told me to ask God for what I wanted. Something amazing came over me. Without knowing what I would say, I opened my mouth and the words "Consume me!" burst out. I dropped to my knees with the fire of God all over me. I cried like a baby right in front of that teenager.

When I asked God to consume me, I asked from a part of my heart I had vaulted up. I hadn't allowed myself to need God at that level in a long time. As I asked with my whole being, I dared to hope. I'm glad to tell you I'm still burning from that day. Even now I tear up remembering how wrecked I was. People kept asking me if I was alright for the rest of the conference because I kept crying. I'm talking about shoulder-shaking, loud, baby crying.

Before the conference, I didn't recognize how much I needed God. I learned to cope with little faith and little fire. It's funny how my disappointment destroyed so many blessings, while quietly stealing my hunger. If you can relate to my story and understand the despair in not trusting God, then please give Him another chance. Allow yourself to hope again.

Loud Hunger

Our hunger's frequency should be louder than we can physically shout. Even when we can't make a lot of noise, nothing can stop our inner man from crying out. There are times I can't stop worshiping God even though it is past bedtime. I go to bed trying to be a responsible grown-up, but the Holy Spirit isn't tired and wants to keep spending time with me. As I'm lying there, my heart continues to burn with praise. He taught me I don't need to make a sound as long as my heart is worshiping. So, in the dark next to my sleeping husband, I mouth prayers like, "I need you, God. I love you, God!" Neil catches me sometimes, and I think it's hilarious.

The Holy Spirit showed me that my sound was heard because my heart was blaring and making some serious ripples in the spirit. One night while I was doing this, I couldn't contain it anymore. I was so on fire I went into my backyard with my iPod and exploded with worship. Then God spoke to me. "Ask Me how much I love you." I was a little self-conscience to speak because up to this point, I had been lip syncing. I didn't want the neighbors calling the cops because they heard a singing burglar in our yard. Looking up at the stars I asked, "God, how much do you love me?" Suddenly, right where my eyes were looking, a meteor streaked across the sky, broke into two pieces, and burned out. I'm pretty sure that was code for "a lot."

God can hear what your heart is saying. A heart that longs for Him can generate a lot of noise, and Heaven will take notice. Just because a person is quiet and hidden to others, it doesn't mean they're hidden from God. Beauty and talent don't fool God. He listens to your heart's signals. If you want to draw Heaven to you, then fire up that hunger. He won't be able to resist you.

The Gospel is for the Poor

Those who are poor in spirit humble themselves and admit they need God. A lot of Christians pretend everything is fine because they want to look godly. But true godly people are repentant and dependent. Many churches have forgotten the focal point of the Gospel: to guide people to repentance, salvation, and God's mercy. The Gospel is God's response to our lack. When leaders emphasize their strengths and mighty works, people assume being a strong Christian is only possible for gifted people. Our message should emphasize our total dependence on Him. We need to remain poor in spirit and wear our vast need for Him as a cloak of humility.

The opposite of poor in spirit is pride. Pride is the same attitude that resulted in Lucifer going rogue. It makes God grieve when He sees people suffer in their own sins while they refuse to ask for help. The Bible says He resists the proud. Don't be a martyr. Ask. You're not bothering God. Remember, He likes to be needed. What He doesn't like is a person who has faith in themselves, which is pride.

One of the last acts Jesus did before the cross was washing the disciple's feet. He grabbed a towel and a bowl of water and knelt down at His friends' feet. They were embarrassed because Jesus was their leader. At first, Peter refused, *"You will never ever wash my feet."* Peter probably expected this would honor Jesus, instead it exposed his own pride. Jesus answered, *"Unless I wash you, you won't belong to me"* (John 13:7-8 NIV).

Jesus has a duel role of master and servant. He doesn't despise our dirty feet and stinky mess-ups; He wants to help us. Jesus did nothing unless He saw the Father do it. The heart of the Father is to take care of our needs. Don't fool yourself. You don't honor God when you bypass His aid. God wants to help us because His cleansing is the only way we can be with Him. Remember, it's the poor in spirit that will have the Kingdom of Heaven.

The Band-Aid

One day, my 9-year-old son, Carter, interrupted my prayer time with a tiny cut on his foot. There was a little blood, but it wasn't bleeding. Looking sad, he came to me needing comfort and reassurance. I told him to go get a Band-Aid, but he wanted me to do it. I enjoyed feeling needed. My retrieval of the bandage helped him feel better, and I was more than willing to go get it. Carefully, I put it on his foot and kissed the Band-Aid. He suddenly felt better, and that pleased my heart.

We need to come to the Father as expectant children and humbly admit our need. Don't tell yourself God considers our bobos beneath Him or He's too busy. Our good Father would stop anything for His little ones.

God's ways are not like man's ways. The world tells us to build up our supply while God tells us to build up our hunger (for Him). The world tells us in order to have power and success, we must earn it or steal it. In the Kingdom of Heaven there's no need to earn your success. God freely gives His power of grace to those who humble themselves. We can't earn what Jesus already paid for.

If you want more of God in your life, then it's time to switch on your hunger. Dig deep into the Word of God. Meditate on how impoverished your soul would be without His mercy. Let your deficiency and need be the driving force behind seeking God. Your poverty of heart will draw all of Heaven. Then God will supply your deep hunger with His deep reserves.

Joy in the Morning

Hunger for God doesn't always manifest as painful cries of desperation. After frequently seeking Him, our desire for Him becomes a joy. In a healthy relationship, a child doesn't constantly beg for his father's love. Our Father in Heaven is faithful and loving. When we hunger after Him, we know He will respond.

Some see God as a distant Father who is still deciding on whether He will love us. This mentality can put us in a cycle of feeling unworthy and unsatisfied. God wants us to hunger after Him and be *confident* He will answer. A holy appetite is one that is full of faith and no condemnation. "I'm not enough, and that's a wonderful thing because that means He will show up." Let's switch on our full dependence, and amp up our hunger signals. God wants to fill our poverty in spirit. The greater deficit we have, the more room He can fill.

Homework

What dreams do you have today? If it's hard to think of any, is it because you've stopped trusting God? Examine your heart and check your level of need for God. If you're not sure you're hungry for Him, then it's time to ask God to increase your level of hunger. Read Psalms 27.

‑‑∿∿‑‑

CHAPTER 6

Silence The Critic

Then King David was told, "The Lord has blessed Obededom's household and everything he has because of the Ark of God." So David went there and brought the Ark of God from the house of Obededom to the City of David with a great celebration.

(2 SAMUEL 6:12 NLT)

King David's passion for the Lord was peculiar for a king. In those days God's presence dwelt with the Ark of the Covenant, which was a holy chest overlaid with gold and topped with two golden statues of cherubim. Since God's Spirit surrounded it, if some-one touched the Ark they would instantly die. As you can imagine, this made it tough to move from place to place.

In 2 Samuel 16, David decided to bring the Ark to Jerusalem with an enormous company of priest and worshipers. As they carried the Ark led by trumpet-ers and worshipers, they stopped every six steps to build an altar and burn sacrifices. By the time this parade approached the city, David was beside him-self dancing and praising God. He threw all decorum out the window by taking off his kingly garments and dancing in his linen undies. It didn't matter he was a king; he was a child of God first. It's impossi-ble to celebrate God with your whole heart and look dignified too.

David placed so much value on the presence of God, he didn't regard his own reputation. Sadly, Da-vid's wife was critical of him. She rebuked him for dancing in front of servant girls. David replied, *"I will become even more undignified than this"* (2 Sam-uel 6:22 NIV). Needless to say, the marriage didn't go well after that.

Here Comes the Critic

As we tune in to God and seek the things of Heaven, we will encounter the *critic*. The critic may be a strang-er or someone you know. Sometimes it's our inner voice controlled by the fear of people's opinions, which is pride. The critic will judge our spiritual experiences and test our level of humility.

Keep in mind, people are *not* the enemy, but unknowingly they can be used by the enemy. We must remember our battle with a critical attitude is not physical but spiritual (Ephesians 6:12). We can only win if we clothe ourselves with humility (1 Peter 5:5).

If there is pride in our hearts, then the critic will have power over us. We can't allow the opinions of others to stop us from pursuing the deeper things of God. If we do, then we can go no further spiritually than where we already are.

Often a critic will pop up when we're starting to experience a new level of freedom. Like David's celebratory dance was criticized by his wife, our exuberant passion for God will be the target of the enemy.

If you plan on aligning with Heaven's frequency, then your heart must first be prepared for the inevitable critic. Consider yourself warned that people pleasing must not be present in you, if you want more of God's glory.

Shed Your Status

The presence of God is not the place to protect your status. It doesn't cost you anything to look regal every time His presence comes. If you're a quiet worshiper who doesn't move a muscle, that's fine, as long as it's not fear of man keeping you quiet.

Don't tell yourself you need to be the mature person in the room, who exudes wisdom and restraint, thus removing any risk of drawing attention to yourself. This is just an excuse to maintain your dignity. Do you want people to be impressed with you or God? Who's the one getting the glory here? Sometimes humbling ourselves means crying, kneeling, raising our hands, shouting, or dancing. Giving God our all is worth any embarrassment.

Frequency of Pride

Pride alters the dial on our spiritual radios. The voice of God becomes silent, and our prayers sound like dead air to Him. He can't hear us because we turned from the frequency of love to the frequency of pride. Pride is so revolting to Him that He shuts off the connection (James 4:6). We convince ourselves that worrying about what others think is being considerate, but the fear of man is a form of pride. Most of the reasons we hold back in worship comes from the enemy trying to silence us.

The frequency of pride has its own broadcast, and it needs to be cast out! When we listen to the fear of man, fear of rejection can slip in followed by offense and jealousy. This is the kind of stuff that goes on when we protect our dignity above love.

Just as two stations compete for the same channel on our car's radio, the enemy will do anything he can to disrupt Heaven's frequency. During worship he will throw prideful thoughts our way. Instead of feeling condemned, recognize his tactics and tell pride to go in the name of Jesus.

Worship and Romance

Worship is a lot like romance. According to the Oxford Learner's Dictionary, the definition of "romance" is *love or the feeling of being in love.* I believe this definition is incomplete. From literature, movies, and perhaps experience, we instinctively know a true romantic act also has a measure of risk.

It's risking your ego by kneeling on one knee, writing a love note with open emotions, and it's singing your heart out when you haven't taken any voice lessons. Like David's wild dance, these gestures subject yourself to possible rejection and embarrassment for the sake of the one you love.

With all this in mind, I believe a more thorough definition of romance is *love accompanied with humility,* because we risk a measure of humiliation when we're being romantic. Taking a risk in worship is similar. It takes guts and vulnerability to sing with your entire heart in church. But I have good news for you—God will love it.

Silence the Critic

Like David's wife, we'll step outside of God's favor if we judge something He blesses. It's easy to judge from an outsider's point of view. Recently I heard a guy argue, "You've got to have balance. Some people have no emotions during worship while others are emotionally unstable." But I have a problem with this statement. Who can observe what is happening in the worshiper's heart? This critic was focused on emotional displays. He went on to describe his disappointment with the worshipers who looked stiff and the ones who always cried. My advice is we should mind our own business, and we won't run the risk of being like David's wife.

Instead of measuring the worshiper on the spectrum of *emotionless vs. emotionally unstable*, we should measure our own hearts. Remember, a strong love frequency is what's important. So, let's take the risk of giving our all and go against the part of the brain which says, "People are judging me right now." Guess what? If they are, then they're the ones with the problem.

Judgment Brings Judgment

Having a critical spirit will stop Heaven's frequency in our lives. We should always stay on guard against self-righteousness taking root in our heart. A self-righteous person or group believes their way of worship is the best worship. They judge others using themselves as the standard.

I know someone else who feels this way. He's Lucifer, God's ex-worship leader. This musical angel was banished from Heaven for thinking too highly of himself. It's prideful to assume our way to worship is the greatest. True worship comes from our spirit, so how can we possibly see the amount of worship someone is expending. If we're having a hard time watching people cry or dance in worship, then we might have a judgmental heart.

God cursed David's wife with barrenness because of her judgmental comment. He didn't want that kind of negativity reproducing. When we permit ourselves to judge, we are killing off that area of our lives from producing life. The last thing we want is for our worship to become something God resists. We must guard our thoughts and words. People who judge others may find themselves barren in their life or in their ministry.

Good Judgment

Judging between sound doctrine and false teaching is different. If you are sitting under someone's ministry, it's important to determine if they are uttering truth. This kind of judgement guards our souls. When someone is speaking into your life, they affect your destiny. Whether or not you know it, their words are influencing your heart and path. Listen to what the Holy Spirit tells you about that person. Also, use the Bible to conclude if something is truth. If it doesn't align with the Gospel of Jesus Christ, then don't receive it!

"Not in" vs. "Against"

There is a misunderstanding many Christians have. Because of this, they judge and miss fresh moves of God. The mentality that "if it's *not in* the Bible, then it's not of God" is a man-made concept. I've got news for you. The Bible doesn't have every miracle God can perform listed in it. I don't know where this theology started, but it's faulty. It puts the Almighty God in a closed box. Rather, we should ask ourselves, "Does it go *against* what the Bible says?"

John tells us Jesus did many other mighty acts. If every one of them were written down, he supposed even the whole world would not have room for the books (John 21:25). There are countless miracles Jesus did that we haven't heard about. Jesus did more than walk on water (John 6:19), turn water into wine (John 2:9), translate to different locations (John 6:21), fly up to Heaven (Acts 1:9), open blind eyes with His spit (Mark 8:23), walk through a wall (John 20:26), raise himself from the dead (Matthew 28:6), literally glow (Luke 9:29), talk to the spirits of Elijah and Moses (Luke 9:30), sweat blood (Luke 22:44), cast demons into pigs (Mark 5:13), and interacted with angels (Matthew 4:11).

Furthermore, Jesus told us we would do greater things than He did. That is in the gospels, my friend. This makes the possibilities for miracles limitless. For our own protection, it's wise we hold our tongue and reconsider speaking against revivals, signs, and wonders. We must ask ourselves if they are going *against* the Bible and search for the positive or negative fruit (outcome).

Let's not judge a move of God from gossip and speedy conclusions because bad news travels faster than truth. Instead of reacting to one-sided stories, we must research it.

Also, it's essential we ask the Holy Spirit what He thinks, and wait for His response. We shouldn't rely only on our own reasoning. Before judging a sign, wonder, or miracle that doesn't fit in our theology, let's ask the Holy Spirit to speak to us about it. We wouldn't want to hinder God's presence in our own life because of hasty judgments.

Judging Because It's Weird

God is supernatural, which seems weird and unusual to our human intelligence. Why do most people of "civilized cultures" assume God will bring revival to only the ones wearing suits and ties during Sunday service hours? Our concept of God should match what is in the Bible. Just open it and you'll read of angels with eyes covering their wings and bodies, John visiting Heaven and eating a scroll, and Moses' face glowing like a light bulb. Come on, people. I can't be the only one reading this crazy stuff.

The Word tells us Jesus is a stumbling stone (1 Peter 2:8). Why? Because He's weird to us. He will challenge our perspective on reality. Jesus told us things like, *"For my flesh is real food, and my blood is real drink"* (John 8:55). By the way, if you're on the subway and the guy next to you says that, run! When you signed up for this Christianity thing, you made this wild Man your Lord and Savior. What's more astonishing is God wants us to be like Him!

Judging through Self-Righteousness

When I was 17 and on a mission trip in Mexico, God opened my spiritual eyes. I saw demons in the crowd trying to hinder the Gospel from reaching the people. I shared with my team, and encouraged us to pray. Another girl in my group stopped our leader and said, "I don't get it. Why didn't I see the demons? I don't think it happened. I usually see that kind of stuff." Her words sounded self-righteous.

Our leader ignored her protest since everyone in the group felt the spiritual resistance I described. We prayed, and our discouragement lifted because we understood the enemy was putting up a fight for good reason. Unwilling to give up, we continued to witness to the crowd and saw people receive Jesus.

Today I understand it was just a teenager showing immaturity. I'm sure she's changed by now. This story is an example of how self-righteousness will try to hinder us from receiving God's blessings through other people. Just because God hasn't given you the sign and wonder first, doesn't mean it's not real. Being able to hear from God is not a guarantee He will tell you all the revelation He told everyone else. This is a self-righteous attitude.

Rule-Breakers

The Pharisees were self-righteous and jealous when Jesus showed up in their town with his radical teachings and crazy miracles. Jesus was a rule-breaker when it came to man-made rules. He didn't make his disciples wash their hands before eating, which infuriated the Pharisees. Also, He healed people on the Sabbath, which, according to religious leaders, broke the fourth Commandment. But in actuality, it was one of the 600+ rules amended to the Ten Commandments they were defending. The Pharisees' legalistic interpretations of the law skewed from the intent of the law. If we look closely at the Bible, we see that God loves to break man-made protocols. It's His way of humbling us and stretching our paradigm.

The bottom line is there will always be people ready to judge. God watches how we react to their scrutiny. Let's shed off the *fear of man* and put on the *fear of the Lord*. When we worship, let's do it as if we are before His throne because we are!

Broadcast your worship beyond your immediate atmosphere and trust God is your listening audience. Ignore the critics, including the one in your head. How much status are you willing to risk for God's glory? It's time to become undignified like King David, so your love-felt worship can be heard in Heaven.

Homework

If there are moves of God you have come against, then it can hinder God's frequency in your life. I encourage you to check your heart for self-righteousness or jealousy and then ask these three questions.

1. *Does it go against the Bible?*
2. *Is the fruit/outcome of the movement positive or negative?*
3. *What does the Holy Spirit say about this?*

After examining your motives, looking at scripture, observing the fruit, and listening to the Holy Spirit, you should have a clearer perspective on the move. If you can see it's of God, then repent for speaking against the works of God. Say, "I nullify and break any words or word curses I've spoken against it. God, I ask that you will remove the curse of barrenness from my life, in Jesus' name."

‑‑ᶰᶵ᷍ᶰᶵᶰ‑‑

CHAPTER 7

Radiating His Presence

After suffering humiliation and torture, Jesus held on to life until He knew it was finished. Moments before His death, He gave the enemy one last blow. His final breath of life departed in a loud cry (Mark 15:37-38). At that moment the temple veil, which separated the Ark from mankind, ripped from top to bottom. This was a tremendous feat since the curtain's thickness was four inches of layered cloth. According to scriptures, there was an earthquake. I like to think the last shout produced by the Creator and Word Himself sent out a supernatural shockwave causing a quake which resonated as far as the depths of Hell.

This cry was His last act of love before His death. Instantaneously, the barrier between us and the Father tore as the cry from Jesus' heart carried out Heaven's frequency. This was the culmination of Christ's life on Earth. He constantly removed the obstacles that separated people from Him. Since the beginning of time, the Creator has stopped at nothing to reach His ultimate desire, which is unity with His children.

Temple of God

> *Don't you realize that all of you together are the temple of God and that the Spirit of God lives in you?*
> *(1 CORINTHIANS 3:16 NLT)*

In Jesus' time, Jews traveled long, dusty distances to pray and offer sacrifices at the temple. The common citizens didn't have permission to enter the outer courts, much less the room with the Ark. Only the priests had that privilege. Once a year the High Priest would prepare himself through cleansing rituals to enter this room, the Holy of Holies. The cleansing rituals were vital because if they weren't done properly, the priest would die when he entered the room with the Ark. God's presence *cannot* allow any sin.

I'm so glad Jesus tore the veil. Being a Gentile woman with no animals to sacrifice, I could never have visited the outer courts of the temple, much less the Ark. Jesus' blood has the power to cleanse us and make us holy. When the curtain ripped, the Holy Spirit no longer required a room. People washed in His blood became temples for Him to dwell. Unity with His children was finally possible!

Walking Temples

Because we are temples, we carry His presence with us. We have no obligation to journey afar to pray in a designated building. Now we can worship Him in our cars, beds, closets, anywhere. We don't walk to temples; we are walking temples.

Once I tried to explain to a Muslim why it was okay if we had a potluck dinner in our church. He didn't understand. In his religion, the mosque is a holy place for worship, and a casual luncheon within it would be blasphemous. I told him we don't need to go to a temple to pray because we are the temple. We can pray to God everywhere we go because we are carriers of His presence! Hopefully, that guy walked away with a greater understanding of God's love and goodness. It's so freeing to know we don't need a building. The Holy of Holies is in our very being. He will never leave us!

Clean Temples

This revelation must change how we live. Knowing God is along for the ride should make us even more aware of what we watch on TV or view on our phones.

Ephesians 4:30 warns, *"And do not grieve the Holy Spirit of God, with whom you were sealed for the day of redemption"* (NIV). When I think of grieving the Holy Spirit I cringe. I'm already sorry Jesus had to die on the cross for my sins. Continuing to upset the Holy Spirit is the last thing I want to do.

Our eyes and ears should be heavily guarded, so we won't grieve Him by cluttering our temples with muck. Everything we do either cleans or clutters our temples. Since we don't want to offend the Holy Spirit, we need to be careful of what enters our eyes and ears.

The window to our soul is our eyes. To be in control of what goes through them is our responsibility. It may be an innocent show we're watching, but the commercials can flash images of the occult, sexual lust, or fear in less than a second. We can blame it on the network, but ultimately, it's our job to censor what enters our soul's window. You may have to turn off your favorite program or walk out of a movie, if you feel your insides cringe. That's the Holy Spirit telling you He ain't having it. If Jesus was sitting on the couch next to you, what would you say in such a scenario? You might say, "I'm sorry you had to see that, Lord."

Profane images and words stick to our souls like poop on a shoe. The stench can hit us at the most inconvenient times. Having ungodly things in you is the same as having false gods in God's temple. You may not be worshiping that stuff, but you *are* trashing God's space with it.

We also need to watch what comes out of our mouths. *"What goes into someone's mouth does not defile them, but what comes out of their mouth, that is what defiles them"* (Matthew 15:11 NIV). Do our words give death or life? If our conversations lean towards negativity, then our heart is not right. This is a clue there is something ungodly we need to repent of and loose from our soul. We want to be an inviting place in which God desires to dwell.

Consecrated Ones

Consecration means we will separate ourselves for His divine purposes. Instead of asking, "What can I do that doesn't offend God," let's ask, "What can I do to please God?" It may sound like a similar question but it comes from different frames of thought. The first question comes from a mentality that the permissible will of God is fine. I'm not saying this is wrong. The thought process here is, "I can do all the things the Holy Spirit allows." This isn't bad, every Christian should follow the leading of the Holy Spirit when making decisions.

But the second approach I'm talking about is more proactive. It asks the questions, "What will please Him most? What does He prefer me to do?" The thought here is to go beyond the minimum requirement to please Him. Like giving a gift when it's not His birthday, our eager consecration will show Him our affection. For example, I know there are movies that are borderline. He wouldn't correct me if I started watching them, but I also know He isn't asking me to watch them.

Proactively pleasing God is different from being dogmatic. There's no need to put self-imposed rules of dos and don'ts on yourself. Living such a rigid life will only end in self-condemnation. Instead, let's be intentional with keeping our souls filled with the love and life of God. I encourage you to guard what you let into your soul with the goal of pleasing God.

Loose It

Sin and shame can clutter our souls, which makes receiving Heaven's frequency near impossible. Jesus is the only one who can clean up our mess. His blood is powerful enough. To clean up any disasters we've made, we should repent and ask for forgiveness. Thankfully, we can trust He will wash our sins away.

Sometimes, we have the problem of sin remaining in our memory. It would do us no good if our sins kept playing like movies in our minds. The devil can use these thoughts to toy with us. Here's an example of how I pray over my soul. Say, "I choose as an act of my will to loose all the ungodly images, profane words, violence, fear, and sounds which are not pleasing to You. I loose it from my soul in Jesus name." (I learned this from a minister named Kat Kerr, and she calls it a "soul check.") Just like when we give Him our pain, we can give Him the thoughts and memories in our souls that grieve Him. Living in the world today, you may have to pray like this daily.

His Habitation

It's been called many things: the secret place, the temple, God's dwelling place, the Kingdom of Heaven. Whatever you want to call it, it's in you. You carry the Kingdom of Heaven within your being because God literally inhabits you. I'm not talking about a tiny piece of God; our spirit houses all of God Himself.

I once heard someone describe it like this, God has an unlimited number of layers. When we accept salvation, it's like we receive a layer of Him. Each layer contains all of who He is. We aren't getting a part of Him, but all of Him. This is how God can be everywhere at once. We also have layers. That's how we can be on Earth and seated in Heaven at the same time (Ephesians 2:6). Our human understanding of spiritual things is limited, but I believe thinking of God as having layers is one way we can wrap our minds around how God is in so many places and in so many people at once.

Including God

How would we live if we could see the King of kings living inside us? We might acknowledge Him a lot more throughout the day. We can't always break out into a worship session or cry out to God in intercession, but we can remain aware of His closeness. When our hearts and thoughts involve Him, then we are living life with Him.

I can feel when there is sin or clutter separating me from the Holy Spirit. There's no need to spend hours repenting and fasting. I just repent if needed and pray in the Spirit under my breath until I feel Him again. Immediately reconciling with God makes being a Christian so much easier. Trust me, the longer you wait to repent and make things right with God, the harder it is to do.

Some people believe God only has time for the important things in a person's life, but I disagree. He's in you, waiting all day for you to seek Him. You might have a hard time believing this, but think about it. Is there a time during the day when God steps out to take a break? Didn't we learn He is a faithful God? The reason this is so hard to believe is humans usually only experience conditional love. It's astonishing to us that our Heavenly Father loves us and is with us at *all* times.

Include God in your day-to-day activities. He cares about the details you care about. At times, I have mentioned to God in our ongoing conversation that I liked something; and by the end of the day, someone gave me the item as a gift. I'm talking about specific items like a white button-up shirt with gray stripes or a new pair of blue running shoes. I didn't ask for those things; I just thought of them. By keeping God close, I have His favor. Just like a good father, He's looking for ways to let me know He loves me.

Changed Atmosphere

The more time you spend with God, the more aware you become of His Spirit inside you. Spending quality time with God grows the relationship. As you grow in God something else happens. Your passion for Him becomes contagious. The Kingdom of God, which is love, joy, and peace, will spill out of you onto those around you. You will change the atmosphere in a room as you carry the presence of God.

The apostles knew they carried the Holy Spirit, and they lived like it. Have you ever been around a powerful man or woman of God and sensed the Holy Spirit just by being in their proximity? I have. I once went to go see David Hogan minister. We were in a church worshiping, when suddenly I felt so overwhelmed by the Holy Spirit, I almost fell. I thought to myself, *There is something behind me.* I turned and sure enough there was Bro. Hogan praying for someone.

Another time, I was visiting a church where revival was happening. I could hear a group of women praising God and laughing in the bathroom. I thought it was awesome. But while I felt the Holy Spirit, I wasn't as affected as them. I went into the main sanctuary and began meditating on God. Suddenly, an intense wave of God hit me, and I became so inebriated I could barely move. I realized the women had spilt out of the bathroom and were fumbling into the room. I was in the front row while they were coming in about 50 feet away from me. The presence of God on these little church ladies drastically changed the atmosphere in the entire sanctuary.

God's presence is tangible. People can feel it whether or not they recognize what it is. Our hope is for the power of God to be so potent people are delivered when we arrive with Heaven. We are a bunch of nobodies without God. I can't change lives or heal the sick with my power. Thankfully the Holy Spirit takes the pressure of performance off of us. All we have to do is obediently bring Him. When we show up, the God of Heaven's army shows up. What happens next is His choice.

A Coming Day

There is coming a day when the veil between the spiritual Heaven and the physical Earth will lift. A day when every believer will have signs and wonders follow them (Mark 16:17). In Acts 5:15, they lined the sick up so Peter's shadow would touch them and heal them. People recovered because Peter was frequent in His personal prayer life. He would spend so much time with the Holy Spirit that Heaven spilled out of him. Because Peter carried the atmosphere of Heaven, he didn't need to lay hands on them to see them healed.

Today, there's a pastor in Singapore, Jeff Yuen, who takes his church out to the streets every Sunday to pray for people. He said when the crowds get too big, it's faster to use their shadows to heal the sick. One of the girls on his outreach team is short and couldn't do much with her little shadow. So, she started bringing a large umbrella to extend her shadow. She tells the people to go under her umbrella, and they are healed! Isn't that amazing? You can find this church at soakability.com. They spend hours soaking in the presence of God in order to operate in that kind of power.

I know I'm not the only one who longs to see every believer healing the sick and setting the captives free. While some people flow in the miraculous, I'm hoping for a day when it becomes the mark of every Christian. When Jesus left us here on this Earth, He left hoping we would catch the fire of the Holy Spirit. It's this fire which heals and delivers. As we spend time tuned in with Him, we ignite on the inside. So, keep praying, soaking, and reading the Bible!

Elisha was a mighty prophet of God who did little, old things like multiply oil and raise the dead. He was so full of the Spirit of God that long after Elisha died, the power on his body was still potent. Once when some Israelites were burying another man, they saw some raiders coming. They tossed the dead man into Elisha's tomb and ran. When this body touched Elisha's bones, he became alive and jumped to his feet! That power was just the leftovers of a devoted life spent pursuing God.

Prioritize Consecration

The prophet Elisha was so occupied with seeking God, he often communicated through messengers. His prayer life had razor-sharp focus, and he knew exactly what he needed—the face of God. He wouldn't allow other people's urgent situations dictate his actions. When people asked for him, he would send messengers, who were most likely prophets he mentored. I'm sure he would have loved the convenience of a cell phone. Very few times did he do something without first trying to resolve it with a text... I mean messenger. He prioritized spending time with God so much that when his friend, the Shulamite woman, came to ask for her son to be resurrected, he tried to send one of his guys. But that momma wasn't going to accept it. Elisha went to her home and stretched out over the boy three times and cried out, *"O Lord my god, please let this child's life return to him"* (1 King 17:21b NLT). Miraculously, the child came back to life.

This is a hurting world which yearns for the Kingdom of Heaven. And guess what? We are it. I'm sure many people thought Elisha was weird for always praying and sending messengers on his behalf. He consecrated himself away from anything that blocked his reception of God's signals. We must prioritize staying in communication with Heaven like Elisha did. Why? Because Elisha heard the voice of God, walked in the miraculous, and was untouchable to the enemy. In other words, staying in tuned with Heaven's frequency was a matter of life and death to Elisha and to those around him.

How much are you willing to sacrifice for God's presence? How much time would you invest if you knew you would clearly hear His voice? People might have called Elisha a weirdo, but when they had a crisis, they sure were knocking down his door. He was a carrier of the power and presence of God, and we have something Elisha didn't have, the revelation of Jesus. We are equipped with much more authority than he had. Our possibilities are limitless. It is time we wholeheartedly pursue God and learn to follow the leading of the Holy Spirit who dwells in us. Who's with me? Are you ready to radiate His presence?

Homework

Ask the Holy Spirit if there are any things you have been letting into your temple that grieves Him. *Repent* and *loose* those things from your soul. By doing this you remove the unwanted trash which blocks the voice of God. This will be helpful as we go into the next chapter about dialing in to Heaven.

-∿-

CHAPTER 8

Dialed In To Heaven

For our citizenship is in Heaven, from which we also eagerly wait for the Savior, the Lord Jesus Christ.
(PHILIPPIANS 3:20 NKJV)

Congratulations! When you became a child of God you gained citizenship to Heaven. You've probably heard that you're a citizen of Heaven before, but how could this possibly help you while you're here on Earth? Other than walking around and bragging to everyone you're a citizen of Heaven, what else could you do with that information? Jesus told His followers they were a part of the Kingdom of Heaven with every chance He had. Knowing you're a citizen of Heaven is more than just a confidence booster; it's the secret to victory.

Heaven is an active place teaming with angels, saints, and (best of all) God. As we tune in to love, we get on the same frequency as Heaven. Each time we allow our desire for Him to transport us before the throne, He equips us for what's coming. Heaven has reserves of supernatural intel, strength, anointing, peace, joy, and much more to carry out our missions.

Throughout the Bible when people encountered Heaven, they received the resources they needed for their current season. I'm talking about game-changing breakthrough. Jacob received a blessing and favor when he encountered the ladder to Heaven. John picked up insight, warnings, and promises when he spiritually visited Heaven while on the island of Patmos. David gained battleplans, songs, and the blueprint of the temple. The exact resource needed to turn the tide is sitting there in Heaven, and as citizens we *need* to possess it.

Where is Heaven

Some say Heaven is in outer space while others say it's in an alternate dimension. I'm not sure, but what I *do* know from the Bible is Heaven exists in multiple places at once, just like God. As Christians we are ambassadors of Heaven and commissioned to carry Heaven wherever we go. Smith Wigglesworth was a man who carried the power of Heaven. The miracles he performed were jaw-dropping because he stayed connected to Heaven. He once said, "I don't often spend more than half an hour in prayer, but I never go more than half an hour without praying" (Hibbert 32). He understood Heaven is never further than a prayer away.

When Jesus evangelized on this Earth, He continually taught the Kingdom of Heaven is here. I mean, He really went on and on about it. Heaven was the good news which compelled Him to share at every chance. Most people assumed because He was the Messiah, He would fight off the Romans and build His palace in Jerusalem. Instead, He was building the Kingdom of Heaven in people. The humans were wrong, as usual.

Jesus spent His life telling everyone there's good news, but most didn't get it. He labored in love to reveal Heaven to a bunch of clueless people. Heaven is a joyous place full of splendor, and it surpasses anything mankind can fathom. If we could see the wonders Jesus saw, we wouldn't stop talking about Heaven either. When Jesus said, "The Kingdom of Heaven is here," He was saying through Him we have access to Heaven now!

I'm in Heaven and Heaven is in me. Try wrapping your brain around that mind twister. Boy, the supernatural doesn't follow any of our understanding of space and time. Even though His realm is outside of what we can physically see and hear, we can trust it is near. It takes faith to believe Heaven can fit in our small beings, but once we do, imagine the confidence and authority we will operate in.

Heaven Encounters

Each time we tune in to Heaven it will be different. Sometimes it's like swimming in liquid love, while other times God will bring correction and restoration. Tuning in to Heaven's frequency means God may communicate to us anyway He likes. We may experience a vision, which is seen by our spirits, or an open vision, which is more like watching a panoramic movie displayed in front of us. On rarer occasions people have out-of-body visits to Heaven. In these encounters the person is no longer just a viewer but a participator in a reality which seems more tangible than on Earth.

Every so often Heaven comes to us in a cloud of glory or a visit from an angel, but the more common encounters are through dreams and visions. A peaceful sensation or a quick mental image may be all you receive in your prayer time. Don't discount those images; they could be messages from Heaven!

Seek Heaven

> *So, let us come boldly to the*
> *throne of our gracious God. There*
> *we will receive His mercy, and we*
> *will find grace to help us when we*
> *need it most.*
> *(HEBREWS 4:16 NLT)*

Mercy and grace? Now that's something we all can use. The book of Hebrews tells us to come to the throne of God which, by the way, is in Heaven. Since we need God's mercy and grace daily, wouldn't it make sense to go to the throne daily? Life would be hard if I spent no time at home where I can relax in my comfy chair wearing my favorite stretchy pants. It's important to recoup at home, but it's more important we frequently rest in our spiritual home. We know Heaven is our home because Jesus gave us the keys (Matthew 16:19). The Bible also tells us we're currently seated (in a comfy chair) in Heaven (Ephesians 2:6). Sounds like home to me.

> *If you were raised with Christ,*
> *seek those things which are above,*
> *where Christ is, sitting at the*
> *right hand of God.*
> *(COLOSSIANS 3:1 NKJV)*

The Bible tells us many times to seek His Kingdom. But how? Anytime we seek God and His commands, we are seeking Heaven. The Scriptures say we should come like little children (Matthew 18:3). Children are vulnerable, playful, honest, wide-eyed, and eager. My advice is to approach your time with God with as much humility and vulnerability as you can muster. Go against your brain's reasoning which says you're sitting in an empty room talking to nobody. To seek the Father in Heaven it helps to use your child-like imagination to picture the things described in the Bible.

Believe you are on the banks of the golden river of God which flows under the royal-blue throne made of lapis lazuli stones. Imagine the emerald rainbow encircling the seated Father, whose face shines brighter than the sun. The worship from the seraphim, cherubim, living creatures, and saints flows out in waves. Picture Jesus in royal robes seated at the right hand of the Father, whose garment is so extravagant it fills the temple with its brilliant radiance. Visualize the roaring river of fire and the tree of life, which produces the juiciest, most scrumptious fruit for every season.

Heaven is not just a faraway home where you will one day retire; you are already there sitting in your chair. Seeking Heaven is easier when you amp up your faith by thinking on Heavenly things described in the scriptures. Meditate on God's Word until it becomes real to you.

The Tabernacle Prayer Model

Let me take you through the steps I often use to enter the presence of God. This guideline of prayer is not the only model out there, but it works. God revealed it to my Mom after a 40 day fast many years ago. Since then, we've seen others receive similar prayer models from God. The Tabernacle Prayer Model uses the structure of the Tabernacle in the Old Testament as a guide, so we can enter the presence of God with focus.

Step 1: The Gates

The Word tells us to enter His gates with thanksgiving and His courts with praise (Psalms 100:4). When worshipers came to the Tabernacle, they first entered the gate. So, right out the gate (pun intended) I sing my thanks to God. I take time to thank Him for His blood, which makes access to Him possible. Approaching God with an attitude of gratefulness opens a door to Him. It's proper protocol to come to the King with thanksgiving. *"Open for me the gates of righteous; I will enter and give thanks to the Lord"* (Psalms 118:19 NIV).

Step 2: The Brazen Altar

Next, we come to the Brazen Altar where they burned sacrifices. Here I sing praises to God. It helps to know the various titles and roles of God in the Bible, such as the King of Heaven's Armies, Ancient of Days, and the Lion of Judah. There are over a thousand titles for God in the Bible depicting facets of His character. You could keep a running list for yourself as you come across a title or you can find alphabetized lists on the internet. Just the titles beginning with A are enough to last several praise sessions.

I love to sing out who God is in praise because it builds my faith while causing the enemy to tremble. For example, with just one of His titles I'll sing, "You are the *King of Heaven's Armies* and You are seated upon the throne. You rein over all the Earth. Praise to the King whose armies cannot be stopped!" Complimenting and glorifying the Lord like this is called a "sacrifice of praise." Just like the priest sacrificed animals on the Brazen Altar in front of the temple, so *we give our praise as an offering* before the throne. God savored the aroma the animal sacrifices made, just like He loves the aroma of our praises.

Step 3: Laver

Still following the Tabernacle Prayer Model, next we reach the Laver. This is a basin where the priest would wash their hands, symbolizing the cleansing of their sin and guilt. The Laver had mirrors lining the inside of the bowl. At this time of prayer, *we should reflect on our own guilt and repent of any sins*. We need to ask God to search our hearts and reveal any wickedness in us.

I've noticed the first thing which pops in my head after asking is usually His reply. Sometimes He reminds me of a wrong act and sometimes it's just a subtle thought I had in my heart that didn't please Him.

For example, one morning after I asked this, I remembered a text I sent to a friend, which seemed innocent. Instead of ignoring this nudge, I thought about my interaction. Suddenly, I realized I had decided in my heart to stop pursuing our friendship because she had previously rejected me. I repented for being guarded and not allowing myself to be vulnerable by still loving her like Jesus would.

If God shows us something, we shouldn't just say, "I'm sorry." We must admit when we are wrong and make things right. Asking for His blood to wash away every sin makes our conscience spotless. Like the priest at the Laver we can be cleansed and made ready to enter the Holy Place.

Holy Place

The Holy Place is the room before the Holy of Holies. We're getting closer! There are three things within the Holy Place: the *Golden Lampstand,* the *Table of Shewbread,* and the *Altar of Incense.* Here we "set our face" towards seeking God. Sure, we could gain forgiveness and walk away at this point, but that is the attitude of a person who just wants to get by.

I have an example of this from visiting a Catholic church. Now I know this doesn't represent all Catholics, but I was shocked that after the sacrament of communion, half the congregation walked past their seats and out the door. Mass wasn't over, but since many felt they had gained forgiveness, they were okay with leaving mid service. Instead of doing the minimal requirement, let's "set our face" to obey above and beyond.

It's interesting to me that the three features we have on our face are represented in the room of the Holy Place. The Table of Shewbread has fresh revelation and sustenance for our mouths. The Altar of Incense offers the sweet smell of prayer for the nose. The Golden Lampstand gives light, so we can see. These steps awaken our spiritual eyes, nose, and mouth. Each piece of furniture in the Holy Place shows us how to pray with our spiritual senses.

Step 4: Table of Shewbread

After we've repented at the Laver, we'll want to spend time at the Table of Shewbread. Bread symbolizes the Word we consume to nourish our souls. *Here we can read, sing, or proclaim scriptures over our lives.* When a verse seems to jump off the page, I spend my time consuming it until I feel like God has finished speaking to me through it.

Let me give an example, because I think it's important to know how to chew on scripture. Let's use Psalms 24:7 (NIV). "*Lift up your heads, you gates; be lifted up, you ancient doors, that the King of glory may come in.*" I may sing or declare something like this: "**Lift up your heads, you gates.** Stand at attention and lift up your eyes. Open up every part of me. Let nothing be closed off. The gateways of my heart, eyes, soul welcome in the light of glory. Every fiber of my being waits in expectation and is open for the King of Glory. **Be lifted up, you ancient doors.** Listen up you ancient entrances. The doors that have been shut and waiting for such a time as this, open! Now is the hour for God's glory to come flooding in. Old promises, old prayers, old declarations which have been lying dormant, open up! Unlock for the move of God. Open up for an infilling of His royal glory."

I could keep going on like this. It's fun when it turns into a rhyme or a new song. Do you see how thinking like a thesaurus and saying the verse an alternate way will give new insight and revelation into a scripture? The Holy Spirit will direct us as He breathes life into the verses. We could speak that same declaration over people, regions, or long-awaited promises. I imagine this kind of prayer is like baking the bread of revelation.

Step 5: Altar of Incense

Once we've got some fresh revelation, it's time to put it into action. *The Altar of Incense is where we pray for needs.* Our prayers rise like ribbons of incense until they reach Heaven. We can intercede with more faith and authority because we've eaten the bread of God's Word. Here we can pray for others, our country, our church, our family, etc.

However, we shouldn't feel obligated to pray for everything. I only ask for what God puts on my heart. A prayer list isn't wrong, but personally I could never focus when I had one. Sometimes I only pray for one thing, and then I'll get peace that I'm done for the moment. By praying this way, we won't get bored checking off a list or worry if we did enough.

It takes the pressure off when our prayer time follows God's lead. I never want to go back to those times of rushing through my prayer list, so I can do what's next on my schedule. When we feel the Holy Spirit leading us in a direction, we should follow. Those prayers carry breakthrough.

Step 6: Golden Lampstand

Our prayers don't have to be perfect and all-encompassing because we have the Holy Spirit to help us. As we imagine ourselves at the Lampstand, *we should pray in the Holy Spirit* (see Jude 20). When we speak in tongues, we pray God's perfect will over a situation, even when we are unaware of what to say. Also, we give prophetic words and receive instructions only our spirits and the angels can understand. Praying in tongues builds up our spirit and stirs the gifts in our lives. On days when I pray in tongues a long time, I see the best visions and God moves more powerfully. That's just a tip.

Step 7: Holy of Holies

Now we've reached the room in the temple where the Ark sits. This is God's dwelling place, *where we encounter Heaven*. It's the perfect time for soaking. Because we're on holy ground, it's important to be still and listen for the faint whisper of the Holy Spirit. Scriptures call this "waiting on the Lord." Sometimes we may start to doubt He will show up after a few seconds of waiting. That's the flesh working against us. We are so used to pushing a button or touching a screen to get instant results. But as we take the time to wait, Heaven *will* come, and our faith *will* grow.

What will God do after we've waited for a while? I don't know. Sometimes I get an overwhelming sense of love, peace, or joy. Sometimes I hear His voice or see a vision. Sometimes I just get to know Him as a Father. The power and authority we receive when we wait is so much more than what we get when we rush.

Moses waited on God and his face would glow. Jesus waited on God and raised the dead. Elijah waited on God and called down fire. David waited on God and became a victorious king. Do you see the correlation here? Those who learn to wait are unstoppable because they completely depend on God. The devil can crush people operating in their own strength, but not against a surrendered God-seeker. He'll lose every time!

Why Seek Heaven?

> *To this John replied, "A person can receive only what is given them from Heaven."*
> *(JOHN 3:27 NIV)*

To put it simply, Heaven is where you get equipped. You need a prophetic word? Heaven's got it. You need protection? Heaven's got it. You need power? Heaven's got that too! The list goes on. Anything you do in your own strength is not worth doing. A few minutes in the courts of Heaven can have more impact than a lifetime of human effort.

When you understand Heaven is only a prayer away, your citizenship takes on a new meaning. A Christian's directive is to partner with Heaven and stay connected to its frequency. If anyone tries to convince you that you're spending too much time seeking Heaven, don't believe them. "*The effectual fervent prayer of a righteous man availeth much*" (James 5:16 KJV). That's a fancy way of saying "Keep praying; it's working!"

Homework

When you pray it doesn't have to look the same every time, but the Tabernacle Prayer Model is a superb way to guide your prayers when you don't know where to start. I know it's hard for many people to pray for even 5 minutes. When you follow this template, you'll find that praying for 30 minutes becomes a piece of cake. There are other useful prayer patterns out there. This isn't the only way to pray. But if you want to get into the Holy of Holies, I'd encourage you to follow the Tabernacle Prayer Model.

1. *Thanksgiving (Temple Gates)*

2. *Praise (Brazen Altar)*

3. *Repent (Laver)*

4. *The Word: read it, sing it, or declare it (Table of Shewbread)*

5. *Prayer requests (Altar of Incense)*

6. *Speak in Tongues (Golden Lampstand)*

7. *Wait, listen (Holy of Holies)*

~-ıllı~

CHAPTER 9

The Father's
Heartbeat

Maybe you're still not convinced we need to do all this tuning in. After all, we've got to get off our keister at some point, right? Certainly. Living for God requires a lot of action, but the power to do the action comes from waiting on Him. The best waiters are the best doers. You can't rush God; He operates in a different time frame. Jesus is the perfect example of what a life of power looks like. Along with healing and teaching, He was a prayer warrior who spent hours with God. Those weren't waisted hours.

Jesus taught us how to pray in Matthew 6:9, *"This, then, is how you should pray: 'Our Father in heaven, hallowed be Your name'"* (NIV). He started addressing the Father in Heaven immediately. He stayed tuned in to the Father. Jesus would often escape the crowds to pray and seek His lifeline, the Father. The fact that Jesus considered this more important than a crowd of needy people should make us take notice. Jesus said He did what He saw His Father in Heaven do. How could Jesus see the Father in Heaven, if He was as human as us? I trust the Father spoke to Him the same as He speaks to the rest of His children. It's just that Jesus practiced a lot more than us.

Heaven

When Jesus began His prayer, He was mindful of Heaven. It's where He received all He needed. When He multiplied the food to feed 5,000 people, He first looked up towards Heaven (Mark 6:41). He drew on Heaven's power. Perhaps He even waited to see if the Father would permit Him to do the miracle.

Another time, the people brought a deaf and mute man to Him. Jesus put His fingers in the man's ears, spit on His finger, and touched the man's tongue; then Jesus looked up towards Heaven and commanded the man to be healed (Mark 7:34). The moment Jesus looked up was the moment the Father in Heaven empowered Jesus to speak with the Heaven-infused authority needed for the miracle.

The Keys

I will give you the keys of the kingdom of Heaven; and whatever you bind on earth will be bound in Heaven, and whatever you loose on earth will be loosed in Heaven.
(MATTHEW 16:19 NKJV)

Why should we care that what we bind or loose will also happen in Heaven? Why is Heaven even getting involved? When we command chains to be loosed from a person, Heaven receives the message. All of Heaven is now backing your words. The Father on the throne has recognized the authority of Jesus granted to you through salvation, and He rules in your favor. Now you've got the King of Heaven's armies, the endless resources of Heaven, and the authority from Heaven to command those chains to loosen. This is just another amazing perk to being a child of God.

When you pray or worship don't forget to incorporate the keys of Heaven as much as you can. You can bind and loose things in your finances, relationships, health, government, or whatever. It makes little sense to play the victim when we have this level of power. I am grieved when I hear so many Christian songs today which sing from a gloomy place. I understand what it feels like to be in the dumps and cry out to God in desperation, but this defeated attitude in a song will pass to listeners when they hear it. Guard your heart against songs that give glory to depression. What songs are you drawn to? It is a tell-tale sign of whether you choose the perspective of defeat or victory. We need to use the Keys of Heaven and walk in the authority we have. All of Heaven is in our corner. Don't forget it.

Because you have the keys, you can loose ungodly things and bind prosperous things to your body, soul, or spirit. If you're feeling like there's a little, sad, rain cloud over your head, use the keys to the Kingdom. Say, "I loose from my soul all depression, stress, and hopelessness in Jesus' name, and I bind to my soul the peace, joy, and life of God in Jesus' name." Say it with the authority you have through Jesus. When you declare those words down here on Earth, the supernatural is set in motion in Heaven. I imagine your voice being heard in Heaven like over a P.A. system. An angel with a pencil behind his ear calls out, "We've got an order for peace, joy, and life." Then God replies, "Order up!"

Secret Place

Jesus understood how important it is to stay in touch with the Father in the secret place. With unfaltering frequency, we should meet Him daily in the Heavenly realm. This might sound strange, but Isaiah can back me up here. He wrote that God would give us hidden treasures and riches stored in the secret places (Isaiah 45:3).

I believe God desires to meet with us in this safe spot, where we are hidden in Him. David would often go there when he played on his harp in the fields alone. He wrote, *"There's a private place reserved for the lovers of God, where they sit near Him and receive the revelation—secrets of His promises"* (Psalms 25:14 TPT). Once David discovered the secret place he returned with frequency for the rest of his life. Like Jesus, he couldn't get enough.

David was a mighty, victorious king who wanted one thing more than anything else. Money couldn't buy it, and family couldn't provide it. His greatest desire was to dwell with God all the days of his life gazing at the Lord's beauty. I suspect David spent his life seeking those intimate moments in Heaven. I love how the Passion Bible puts it. *"Here's the one thing I crave from God, the one thing I seek above all else: I want the privilege of living with Him every moment in His house, finding sweet loveliness of His face, filled with awe, delighting in His glory and grace. I want to live my life so close to Him that He takes pleasure in my every prayer"* (Psalms 27:4).

It's mesmerizing to be in close communication with the Father. His peace is so unlike anything on Earth. We discover more of His heart as we build a relationship with Him. He has so much peace and love in store for us if we would only learn to tune in.

God won't force Himself on you. When you begin a relationship with Him, it may seem like you are new friends first getting to know each other. But as you meet with Him each day, you will grow closer and share a deeper understanding. Without a doubt, you'll know He adores you and enjoys your quirks and personality. In time you'll feel free to be yourself.

Confident you are a loved child of God, both your identity and your perspective of the Father will shift. Eventually, the relationship will turn from a growing appreciation to a fiery love. You'll be able to go through your entire day filled from the top of your head to the tips of your toes with complete and utter joy. This is something I've consistently experienced.

David used worship to get to the secret place. Music stirs our emotions and moves us into a spiritual realm. As we pour our love out to God, we literally step into His realm. The more we go there, the more attainable it becomes. And the more we stay there, the more the secret place stays with us. Soon you'll have the atmosphere of Heaven surrounding you so much that an afternoon trip to Walmart (especially during the holiday bustle) can be a joyous excursion with the One you love.

Staying in Communication

Everywhere you go God is in you. You can choose to stay in communication with Him or only acknowledge Him sporadically. If you've read the book Song of Solomon, you've been exposed to just a smidge of the burning passion God has for us. He is longing for your attention and wants to sweep you away to delight in each other's love. It excites Him when we say to Him, "I love you, let's spend time together." Often a Christian's quiet time consists of reading the Bible, working down a prayer list of needs, and ending with an "amen". In the next moment, they're off doing their daily tasks, but have missed the best part.

I don't want you to envision God being a desperate puppy following you around, begging for a belly rub. Instead, He longs for a meaningful relationship. He sees when we are hurting, and He hurts more. He knows when we are faced with problems, and He's trying to get our attention to give us the way out. It's hard for Him to watch us live life without connecting to His available resources. He has everything we need waiting for us. If only we would meet Him in the secret place.

My Prayer Closet

Let me share an experience I had in the secret place, to give you a clear example. One time in my closet, I was pursuing God by worshiping and praying in the Spirit. I simply asked Him to take me to Heaven. I didn't physically go there, but by faith I believed I was there in the secret place with Him. In my thoughts, an image of a leaf flashed. I knew it didn't come from my own imagination, so I had a choice. Instead of getting frustrated that a leaf distracted my meditation, I kept my thoughts focused on the leaf and asked Him to show me more.

Next, I saw the leaf on an enormous tree with blossom-covered branches. Keeping my mind on that image, I asked God to tell me what the tree was. He told me I was the tree. Then I caught a glimpse of Jesus waiting for me next to the tree's thick trunk. I noticed the tree was growing upward, and as new branches formed, more pink blossoms sprouted on them. I understood by the Holy Spirit each blossom was potential fruit (souls). He was showing me the harvest of souls I will eventually reap for the Kingdom. The growing tree meant my prayer life was increasing the amount of people that will ripen to spiritual maturity.

This whole time I felt wave after wave of love and joy. Then in a flash, I got another image of Him handing me a key, so I imagined myself taking it from His hand and eating it. Then I questioned, "Whoops, should I have done that?" I don't know why I ate it. But then He reassured me He wanted me to do that.

Not long after, He drenched me with a powerful sense of urgency. Feeling burdened, I wept for this book, the very book you're reading. As I wept, I couldn't stop saying, "It's the heart of the Father. It's the heart of the Father." In that moment, He shared His deep longing for those blossoming souls to come and fellowship with Him in the secret place.

I believe that in my time hidden in a prayer closet, I received a key to release the heart of the Father through this book. So many people in this world today have an emptiness in their hearts. They ache for a loving father. Whether our dad is the best, worst, or whatever, an earthly father will never fill the void. In reality, we hunger for our Heavenly Father.

It's the Father's desire to let us know that when He created the Earth, we were in Him and were known by Him. He breathed us out into our earthen bodies and has since yearned to reconnect with us. He won't force us to pursue Him because He wants us to love Him by our own choosing. You might be dirty from sin or mangled by life, but to Him you're a sight for sore eyes. His protective arms are burning to give you a big bear hug, but He's waiting for you to ask. Go ahead and ask right now.

Homework

Ask the Father to show you how much He loves you. Spend time meditating on His love for you. Then answer these questions.

1. *Do I fully believe and accept God's love? (Romans 8:38-39)*

2. *What was God doing during the times when I was hurting?*

3. *What does the Bible say about the broken hearted? (Matthew 5:4, Psalms 34:18)*

4. *How did He feel during the times I celebrated in life?*

5. *Has God done anything recently to show me He loves me?*

CHAPTER 10

The Sound Of Angels

I will never forget the time God took me to visit Heaven. I can't write a book about Heaven without sharing my adventure, so here's how it began. At the time, I was 22 years old and dating my future husband. My mind was occupied with upcoming marriage plans more than with God, but that was about to change.

It was a normal night in Arcola, Louisiana, and I was having a nice (Cajun) dream. In the dream, I was among church friends, digging through a sack of Mardi Gras beads which we had caught from parade floats. Without warning, angelic singing invaded the dream.

The glorious voices grabbed my attention because the music was more real than any reality I've known. I don't know how else to explain it. At this point, I knew I was in a dream because while I watched the dream play out, I heard music coming from somewhere supernatural. I hunted for the origin of the singing but only found my unaware friends deep in conversations which seemed to be muted. All I could hear and care about was the worshipful singing of a Heavenly choir. I had to find the source.

Looking to the sky, I spotted an unusual full moon. It didn't appear to be a part of my dream, as it gleamed in high definition. Suddenly, chills ran down my spine. It dawned on me something beyond reality was seeping into my dream. With heightened senses, I braced myself for anything, including death. When I locked my curious eyes on the moon, I lifted up and out of my dream. Passing the atmosphere, I crossed into space. At this point the dream ended, and I was in reality. Wondering how I could maneuver through space so well, I discovered Jesus was behind me, carrying me.

I felt safe as we traveled along a semi-translucent road winding through outer space. The road looked like a floating walkway from the cartoon, *The Jetsons*. We passed a building with Greek columns. Jesus told me the building was a research center where people can study the universe. Then we entered a bright room with a white staircase. I noticed I was going up the stairs, but my feet weren't touching the steps. Jesus was still carrying me. As we approached the top, I could see angels busily walking back and forth. They had wings and wore sashes, each a distinct color. I wondered why they were too busy to notice me, and instantly, I knew they were busy preparing for the return of Christ on Earth.

In the distance, there was one angel standing at attention, and he looked serious. He was guarding a massive, white wall which I sensed was between me and Heaven. I wanted to get past that powerful angel, but doubted I could. Unfortunately, my life was not a shining example of godliness during that time, so my conscience became keenly aware of my sin in the presence of such holiness.

I never mustered the guts to turn around and see Jesus, but I *did* see the Father. As I was taking the whole scene in, He appeared as a bright light in the sky. No one had to explain what the bright light was because I instantly knew. The Source of all love and authority was before me, and He felt like home. He commanded, "Tell as many people as you can about this place."

Boom! I then heard the loudest thunder clap! I felt the sensation of falling for a second then I jolted awake, as if I fell back into my body on my bed. I felt the supernatural realm still in my room but sensed it was covered by only a thin veil. For the first time I realized the spirit world has always been just inches away from our reality. I thought, *Heaven is in this place*. With a healthy dose of holy fear, it took several minutes before I could move a muscle. Even then I wouldn't dare leave the safety of my covers.

90 Minutes in Heaven

For weeks after the trip to Heaven, I heard angels singing with me when I worshipped God in my home and when I played on the worship team. One Sunday our drummer heard an additional backup singer, and he knew it was an angel. Other than him, no one else noticed the singing. I didn't connect the angel voices with the trip to Heaven until a couple of months later, when I went to a college Bible meeting where Don Piper was the guest speaker. He wrote the book *90 Minutes in Heaven*.

The book tells the story of how Don died when a truck slammed into his car. Rescue workers pronounced him dead on scene. The wreckage caught the attention of a couple driving by. As Dick Onarecker and his wife pulled up to the accident, the first responders told them a man had died. Dick felt God urge him to pray for the lifeless body, so he obeyed. Ninety minutes after they declared Don dead, God brought him back to life. Dick was singing a hymn over Don's body when he awoke and joined in the song. Needless to say, Dick was surprised. In his book, Don describes his 90 minutes in Heaven and the people he met there.

That night at the college meeting, I had the chance to speak with him about my dream. He asked me if I could still hear the angels singing. I was stunned because I hadn't told him about the angel voices. He said, "Yep, once you go to Heaven it stays with you. I can still see and hear angels every now and then." This was confirmation I had been to an actual place.

I asked him if he had noticed a large, white wall while he was there. He told me it wasn't a wall. "You saw the Pearly Gates. They go up so high you can't see the top of them." I was ecstatic because I could remember being unable to see the top of the wall/gate. My conversation with Don Piper was a setup from God to confirm to me I had visited Heaven... or rather, Heaven's gate.

Jacob's Ladder

You can imagine my amazement when I came to the story of Jacob's Ladder in Genesis 28. The story starts off with Jacob dreaming, just like my experience. The Bible says a ladder appeared, but I wonder if he saw stairs instead. Perhaps the word for ladder was also the word for steps in his language. Similarly, the ladder/stairs reached to Heaven. Jacob saw busy angels moving up and down the ladder while I saw busy angels at the top-level walking in every direction. He beheld the Lord standing above, and in my case, God was above the ground in front of me. Jacob and I both received instructions. While Jacob acquired promises and direction, I was commissioned to tell as many people as I can about this place. (That's what I'm doing right now!)

Like Jacob, I woke up and knew Heaven was in my room. Jacob said, "Surely, the Lord is in this place." Genesis also mentions he was afraid and said how dreadful that place was. I'm right with you, Jacob. That was a scary thing to go through. Finally, the last thing Jacob said caught my attention big time. He said, "This is none other but the house of God, and this is the GATE OF HEAVEN." What! There are too many similarities to our stories, other than his promise of land, descendants, blessings, and God's protection (I'll try not to be jealous). I'm convinced I visited the same set of stairs Jacob saw.

Heaven Visits

In the previous chapter, I emphasized that meeting the Father in the secret place *is* encountering Heaven. But sometimes God will take it a step further and give us a full-on experience. I bring this up because large portions of the Bible were written by people who claimed to see or *spiritually* visit Heaven. The scriptures recount these supernatural occurrences without apology. These events are God given and not to be ignored. As the time draws closer to His return, we will increasingly hear of people encountering Heaven.

Then as I looked, I saw a door standing open in Heaven and the same voice I had heard before spoke to me like a trumpet blast. The voice said, "Come up here, and I will show you what must happen after this." And instantly I was in the Spirit, and I saw a throne in Heaven and someone sitting on it.

(REVELATIONS 4:1-2 NLT)

I'm no expert on taking trips to Heaven where my spirit actually leaves my body because it's only happened once. However, I do have examples from the Bible I want to share. There are at least five men, not including Jesus, who journeyed in the spirit to Heaven, sometimes more than once.

On one of Isaiah's trips he observed God on His throne and the train of His garment filled the place (Isaiah 6). Ezekiel stood before a throne of precious stone, and the Lord's hand fed him a scroll which tasted sweet (Ezekiel 1-3). The prophet Micaiah saw the Lord sitting on His throne asking all of Heaven, "Who can entice Ahab to go into battle against Ramoth-Gilead so he can be killed?" He saw a spirit volunteer to put lies in the mouths of Ahab's prophets (1 Kings 22:19). John the revelator wrote the entire book of Revelations from his trips to Heaven, seeing events thousands of years in the future. Paul was caught up into Heaven and heard things so astounding humans were not permitted to tell (2 Corinthians 12:4).

Permanent Trips

Elijah also went to Heaven in a chariot of fire, but he never came back (2 Kings 2:11). This was more than a *spiritual* trip; it was a *physical* trip. A physical trip to Heaven is so rare only Elijah, Enoch, and Jesus went to Heaven in their bodies. Though the Bible doesn't mention these men went on spiritual trips to Heaven while they were on Earth, it's likely they did.

Another time a permanent trip is mentioned in the Bible is in reference to the rapture. There is coming a time when, in an instant, the last trumpet will sound, and the followers of God will instantly change. Their physical bodies will transform into glorified bodies. In a flash, Christ will gather the bride to meet Him (1 Corinthians 15:52). No one knows when this will happen. It may happen tomorrow or in 300 years. Either way, we should live both ready to go and ready to stay.

Strange in Heaven

A few times in the Bible, the prophets mentioned they couldn't tell us everything they saw or heard in Heaven. Some things are too overwhelming for our earthly minds to fathom. Compared to what we are used to, Heaven is a strange place. I don't know why Christians attempt to package the things of God as "normal" according to the world's standards. I'm talking about angels with animal heads, people eating scrolls, and flying chariots of fire. You won't see that on the Hallmark channel.

I encourage you to do your own research and study what the Bible says on this subject. Knowing this Kingdom exists will help you believe you aren't just praying and singing to dead air. Your voice reaches the ears of the Father beyond any distance. Believing at this moment you are seated there will fill you with a newfound confidence. Don't buy into the lie that

God is "normal" and wouldn't do anything outrageous. Take your perspective of Him out of religion's man-made box and watch what is possible when you encounter the Kingdom of Heaven.

Homework

Read and meditate on Revelations 4. Note how John is taken up to Heaven. He was not only shown the Throne Room but also the future! By studying verses on Heaven, you are building your faith and preparing your heart for the Kingdom of Heaven to manifest in your life. Revelations 4 is a great place to start, but if you're hungry for more, keep seeking out verses on Heaven. *"For everyone who asks, receives. Everyone who seeks, finds. And to everyone who knocks, the door will be opened"* (Matthew 7:8 NLT).

CHAPTER 11

Receiving From Heaven

The hand of the Lord was on me, and He brought me out by the Spirit of the Lord and set me in the middle of a valley; it was full of bones. He led me back and forth among them.... (4) Then He said to me, "Prophesy to these bones, hear the word of the Lord!" (7) So, I prophesied as I was commanded. And as I was prophesying, there was a noise,

*a rattling sound, and the bones
came together, bone to bone.*
(EZEKIEL 37:1, 4, 7 NIV)

I n Ezekiel's vision, God commanded him to speak to the dry bones. When He obeyed, an army assembled before his eyes. These warriors were the nation of Israel, and God wanted Ezekiel to deliver a message to them. I want to point out two things of importance. First, God gave Ezekiel insight from Heaven. Second, Ezekiel had to act in obedience. God speaks to us in many ways, but if we don't act on it, then it's all pointless. In this chapter, I'll reveal how God speaks to us, and how we should actively respond.

Visions for Everyone

It's hard to believe some Christians deny that the Lord still gives us visions today. Recently, I searched the Bible and found at least 104 different people who had seen visions and/or angels. That's not counting the number of visions each individual saw. Zechariah seemed to have visions every day. Visions are in almost every book of the Bible, so why would a believer consider them rare? He is the same God in Zechariah's time as He is today.

In the Old Testament, people depended on prophets to stay informed of what God was saying. A "regular-ole-Joe" never expected to see visions. That was the seer's job. Now that we have the revelation of Jesus and the Holy Spirit, we don't need a prophet to be our way to tune in to Heaven. It doesn't matter if you're young, old, famous, or unknown. The Holy Spirit wants to activate His children's spiritual eyes. So, stop thinking visions are only for ordained ministers. God is not a respecter of persons. He wants to speak to you just as much as the next guy.

Visions in the Everyday

I can remember the first time I saw a vision. I was with a group of people, and we were praying for a teenage girl. As we all prayed in tongues, we waited for God to show us something. I didn't even try. I never had a vision before, so why would God give me one now? (It's usually when we give up control that God steps in.) As I'm praying in the Spirit, a picture of grass flashed in my imagination. Grass! Why was I thinking of grass at a time like this? I scolded myself and continued to pray. It was often difficult for me to remain focused in prayer because of my active imagination. I felt condemned because I wasn't spiritually mature enough to pray for even two minutes without distractions.

Then one guy spoke up, "God is showing me a plush, grassy meadow. I believe He wants you to rest in meadows of peace." The teen got excited because her name meant "grassy meadow." My jaw dropped. I started questioning everything. Had I been seeing visions all along? Had I been beating myself up for nothing? Suddenly, I remembered all the times pictures had flashed in my mind while I prayed (during church services, mission trips, quiet times, prayer meetings). I always thought something was wrong with my ability to focus. That day God used *grass* to kick start my new journey.

Today, my visions still come in flashes. I've learned that when I get a flash, I should wait for the next one. Often the first image makes little sense until God shows the bigger picture in the next glimpse. I can tell it's a vision when the amount of detail and information is beyond what I could invent. For example, I recently saw a fountain. In a split second, I knew it was made of pearl, trimmed in gold, designed with three layers, and intricately detailed. I also felt it was meant for royalty as well as for refreshing the Earth. They say a picture is worth a thousand words, but when God gives a vision, He makes it worth ten thousand.

Dreams

Dreaming is another way God reveals things to us through pictures. When we sleep, our inhibitions and logic are out the window. If you can recall your dreams, then consider yourself blessed. Whether or not you can, it helps to keep a journal next to your bed or on your phone. That way you'll be ready to record it when it's still fresh in your mind. If you only remember parts and pieces, that's okay. Write it down anyway.

Often a dream seems like wild, unrelated events until I write it out. As I organize my thoughts and see it in print, an interpretation usually follows. Sometimes when it's important, God will keep echoing the dream's message night after night until I grasp it.

Recording my dreams helps me discover ongoing patterns. For months I dreamt of old buildings. When I started journaling, it finally dawned on me God was trying to tell me something. He wanted me to know He was going to abandon the old way church had been done. He gave me a heads up for what was about to happen. Weeks later, the church (and world) went into quarantine due to COVID-19. Keeping a prayer journal kept me from being worried for the church. Instead, I was able to pray the will of God with faith.

Every dream comes from one of three places: God, the enemy, or our own subconscious. Whatever the case, we can learn from it. If it's from the enemy attempting to scare us or tempt us, then we've gained insight on how to strategically pray. We might realize we need to put on the armor of God, cast out the enemy, or resist temptation. If our mind is causing the dream, such as showing up at school in our underwear, then we know we're probably harboring shame or guilt. Many people, who have been bruised by this world, have learned to hide their emotions even from themselves. There's nothing like a subconscious dream for exposing areas that need Jesus. In a lot of our dreams there's valuable information we can use.

When we are faithful to record our dreams, it tells God we won't disregard His voice in this manner. He will speak to us this way more frequently, if He knows we'll pay attention. Honoring the dreams He's given us is a form of seeking Him. How many important warnings or revelations have we missed because we didn't pay attention? Let's take the initiative to hear God through our dreams.

> *And afterward, I will pour out my Spirit on all people. Your sons and daughters will prophesy, your old men will dream dreams, your young men will see visions.*
> *(JOEL 2:28 NIV)*

Sensing Heaven

Sight isn't the only sense God uses to communicate with us. We have five primary senses, but neurologists list as many as twenty-one senses (sensorytrust.org. uk). Some senses include the ability to gauge time, feel temperature, and balance. Each sense is a way we can receive signals from God.

Smells

Have you ever been in deep prayer and smelled a strong fragrance which didn't have a source? It could have been God communicating with you. I've smelled myrrh and frankincense during powerful worship services. It was as if someone put it right under my nose. And then in the next breath... nothing.

Why would God do something like that? He's not a God of confusion. I believe He was telling me He was near. The Shulamite bride in Song of Solomon said, *"Who is this sweeping like a cloud of smoke? Who is it, fragrant with myrrh and frankincense and every kind of spice?"* (Song of Solomon 3:6 NLT). Jesus is the person who the Shulamite bride was describing. More than once I've smelled this aroma, and each time I'm delighted. Sometimes, I'll detect roses. This fragrance also reminds me of Jesus, who is the Rose of Sharon in Song of Solomon.

There are more ways God communicates with us through smells. Death and danger have an odor. These scents warn us to be careful and to do spiritual warfare. Smells can also bring to our thoughts a person who needs prayer or encouragement. Paying attention to fragrances opens up more ways God can direct us.

I'm sure you encounter many smells throughout the day (especially if you're raising boys). But how can we tell if it's spiritual or not? If the aroma doesn't have a source, if it was fully present and then suddenly gone, or if the smell brought someone or something to your mind that needs prayer, then God is likely communicating with you.

If I'm on my keyboard worshiping and a fragrance hits me, I'll sing about it. Even right now as I am writing this, I smell a flowery scent which reminds me of jasmine. It's there only when I breathe out and not in. I'm pretty sure my nostrils don't have perfume in them; however, I am filled with the Holy Spirit who has a paradise of lovely aromas.

> *Your inward life is now sprouting, bringing paradise unfolds within you. When I'm near you, I smell aromas of the finest spice, for many clusters of my exquisite fruit now grow within your inner garden. Here are the nine: pomegranates of passion, henna from Heaven, spikenard so sweet, saffron shining, fragrant calamus from the cross, sacred cinnamon, branches of scented woods, myrrh, like tears from a tree, and aloe as eagles ascending.*
> **(SONG OF SOLOMON 4:13 TPT)**

Each of these scents carry a message. When the Lord surprises me with one, I ask what He is saying. If I don't already understand its meaning, I search the Bible or the internet. Once I have a good guess, I ask God to confirm if I'm right. Sometimes He answers immediately, and at other times I'm required to wait. He is always faithful to confirm, usually in creative ways.

AUDIBLE SOUNDS

I probably don't have to tell you that if you hear an audible sound coming from absolutely nowhere, it's likely spiritual. On rare occasions, I hear the audible voice of God, angels singing, and unfortunately, the enemy. Sounds are not as hard to interpret as visions.

Some spiritually sensitive people walk around interpreting all the sounds they hear. I don't recommend that. Not everything you hear is a spiritual message from God. Instead, you should depend upon the direction of the Holy Spirit. He will speak to you through what people are saying or what you hear in your surroundings. Just make sure what you're interpreting is in alignment with the Word of God.

When a sound seems highlighted to you, pay attention. God may point to a particular sound, like the wind, an alarm, or laughing children. I'm often in my own little world when He speaks like this. I recommend going about your business as usual. There's no need to stay in "sound interpretation" mode. It's better to wait for the Holy Spirit to say "Listen."

Inaudible Voice of the Lord

When God speaks to our hearts, we usually don't hear it with our ears. It can come as an emotion, impression, or thought. At other times He imparts a full download of information in a moment's time. I know it's Him speaking because there is no way I could imagine all of that data so quickly.

Our inner voice is similar to the Holy Spirit's voice. The trick is learning when it's coming from you, the enemy, or from the Holy Spirit. There is a feeling or conviction you get when God is speaking to you. I can't fully explain it, but I know it. The Bible tells us His sheep know His voice (John 10:1-18). As you practice listening and obeying, you learn how to tune in to His voice and tune out other voices.

Inaudible Sounds

As a musician and singer, I've learned to hear songs from Heaven. Let me explain. Sometimes, when the worship team is grooving and the Spirit is moving, a unique melody plays in my spirit. This is what the Bible calls a "new song." I'll sing it or play it, knowing God is using it prophetically over someone. Hearing these inaudible songs is easier when my heart is actively loving God and His people. I've heard sounds like choirs, stringed instruments, trumpets, cymbals, and organs. I can tell you for sure the angels really get involved when we worship.

Recently, God started speaking to me in a new way. He gives me a repeating melody to play on my keyboard. As I play each note, I hear an inaudible word in my spirit. I'm so excited to see where He will take me with this. He's even gone as far as speaking to me through the notes of a bird's song. Trust me, I'm not going around trying to interpret every bird I hear. This happened when I was jogging, just minding my business. It was one of those times when God highlighted a sound and said "Listen."

Sometimes God speaks to us by putting a song we already know on our heart. Do you ever wake up with a song stuck in your head? It could be a message from God. If the song in your head is about victory in the battle, then you better get ready for a battle that day. If it's about the good, good Father, then perhaps you need a revelation of the Father's love. Don't discount those songs stuck in your head.

The Rest of the Senses

God can also speak to us through the sense of touch. Sometimes you may feel heat, cold, or electricity surging through parts of your body. This comes in handy when you're praying for someone and heat from the fire of the Holy Spirit touches them. In this case, the sense of touch is confirmation a miracle is happening. There are people who have a certain gift of healing where they feel a pain in their body, which tells them what ailment to pray for in a person. When the pain leaves, they know to stop praying. So, if God has given you that gift, your indigestion might be a call to intercession.

Taste is another sense God can speak to us through. An example in the Bible is when Ezekiel ate a scroll that tasted sweet (Ezekiel 3). Also, Psalms 34:8 says, *"Taste and see that the Lord is good"* (NLT). Even though it's uncommon for God to communicate through taste, don't discount it. When we stay hungry for the voice of God our senses will be sensitive to the unexpected ways God speaks.

Symbolism

If you want to understand the Bible, interpret dreams and visions, and make sense of God speaking through your senses, then it helps to be a student of symbolism. Once you have something you need to interpret, look it up in the scriptures. You can also ask yourself, "What does this symbolize to me?" God will often speak to us with symbols which hold meaning to us personally. Furthermore, you can determine if the symbol is virtuous or evil by the way it's portrayed in the dream or vision. If you still don't understand, look up its meaning. The more symbols you understand from the Bible, the better you'll flow in the language God speaks.

For example: yesterday in prayer the Lord showed me the word "peony" in pink and I knew it had something to do with our relationship. I'm not too familiar with flowers, so I looked it up. After a quick Google search, I learned a pink peony is given to honor a bride because it represents wealth and love. God wanted to honor me and remind me about the riches of our love together. Now, if I ever see or hear from God about a peony flower, I'll immediately know the meaning.

Interpretation

With all these crazy images, smells, and sounds, we'll need to learn how to interpret them correctly. Don't rely too much on your own knowledge. I know I just told you to learn what symbols mean, but in the end, the Holy Spirit is the only one who can give you true discernment. Ask God for the interpretation (1 Corinthians 14:13). If He doesn't answer, search the scriptures. After examining the Word, you might need to give it your best guess and wait for the Holy Spirit's reply. He will give you a feeling of "yes, you got it" or "keep trying, something is off." If that doesn't work, ask Him to clarify it throughout the events of your day. He *will* do it.

Sometimes the interpretation is not at all what you would guess. Take Amos Chapter 8, for example. *"What do you see, Amos?" He asked. "A basket of ripe fruit," I answered.* (Oh, how nice! Ripe fruit is a good thing, right? It's in a neat, little basket too.*) Then the Lord said to me, "The time is ripe for my people Israel; I will spare them no longer. In that day, declares the Sovereign Lord, the songs in the temple will turn to wailing. Many, many bodies flung everywhere! Silence!"* Well, that took a dark turn. I would have totally messed it up by telling the people of Israel that God is giving them a good harvest. They would have had no warning before those bodies were flung. Interpreting can be difficult, and that's why we need to depend on the Holy Spirit for help.

Interacting

Some visions and visitations are meant for us to receive something. The storehouses of Heaven hold the resources we need to *accomplish* God's will. Moses received the Ten Commandments, Ezekiel received a scroll, John saw a door to go through, and on it goes.

For years I saw visions of things like keys or swords and just stood there, enjoying the show. How was I supposed to know God wanted me to take the key or sword? He was trying to equip me with the things I needed for that season. Now when I see a glimpse of God holding out something to me, I imagine myself taking it. Sometimes, I'll physically go through the motion of taking it as an act of faith. Looking at what the prophets did in the Bible, we can see they interacted with visions. I can't imagine how many years I spent losing my spiritual keys when all I had to do was willfully take them.

God or an angel may show you a door, which could represent opportunity, new level, or revelation. If something like that happens, don't go with them until you've tested the spirit. Say, "Are you of the Spirit of the Most High God, who sent His Son to die for the sins of this world?" They'll either leave or say yes. Once it's safe, then go through the door.

Also, God may hold out something for you to drink or eat, such as bread or the new wine. If you're in public, just picture yourself taking what God gives you, unless He tells you to physically take it by faith. Then be prepared to get some strange looks.

Hear for Yourself

I'm telling you these things because not many people would. It's kind of scary writing such wild stuff, knowing I'll probably get some criticism. I just wish someone would have told me these things twenty years ago when I was holding my breath waiting to hear God's voice. These Biblical tips are hidden in plain sight. Christians who are prophets and seers know these things already, but they aren't likely to tell people because of how crazy it sounds. When God shows them strange things, they keep it to themselves and just give us the interpretation. We get to hear what God said, but not how God said it. We all should be able to tune in to Heaven's signals. Don't you think? It's essential in this day and age.

There are people born with abilities to see and hear in the spirit. But for most, hearing God is such a mystery. We are unaware of the Heavenly realm because we operate on a different frequency. When I started seeking God, I needed every step spelled out. I had to practice tuning in to love, hungering after God, and soaking in the Holy Spirit. I'm still learning. At least now I know, if I seek the voice of God, I will find it.

> *Follow the way of love and eagerly desire gifts of the Spirit, especially prophecy.*
> *(1 CORINTHIANS 14:1 NIV)*

As you live a life on the hunt for God's messages, you're actively desiring the gift of prophecy. If you receive a vision, interact with it. Search out the symbolism of what you saw and pray for the interpretation. Sometimes a vision or a word comes as pieces of the puzzle. Don't trust your memory to hold on to all the details, write it down somewhere. You may get part of the message in a dream and the other part of the message in a song He highlights to you.

Each time God communicates with you is a precious treasure that should be valued. Your prophetic gift increases in proportion to the frequency you tune in to His frequency. You will be on the cusp of what God is doing and saying. Who said being a Christian is boring? This is the greatest adventure anyone could have!

Homework

Let's practice seeing simple visions. At night before you fall asleep, get in an attitude of prayer. When you're ready, ask God to show you something about tomorrow. Write down any images that pop into your head. During the next day, stay alert for the person, place, or thing you saw the night before. If you find it, then it confirms you were seeing from God.

The first time I did this, I saw a haystack with specks around it. To my surprise, the next day I saw a painting called *Haystacks* by Monet. And sure enough, his famous, dotted, painting style gave the haystack a speckled look like in my vision. That confirmed to me I was receiving from God.

-ılılı-

CHAPTER 12

Peace In The Hertz

At this point we've learned to tune in to Heaven's frequency in our quiet time. The next step is to stay tuned in during trials. We know Heaven's transmissions are riding on radio waves of love. Since our hearts can receive and give His love (Heaven's frequency) out at any time of the day, there's no reason we should break transmission.

Staying in constant connection to God means our lives will be transformed by His anointing. We will look and sound more like Jesus when we stay tuned in to His Spirit. He wants us to be able to leave the four walls of our prayer closets and still be in the peace and presence of Heaven.

While the storms of life are upon us, remaining in God's love is essential. The only way to keep this level of intensity during these times is to remove the box put around our prayer sessions. When we step out of our quiet time, we must continue to include Heaven in everything we do. Let's not end our prayer with an *amen,* but keep the conversation going the whole day.

Living in His frequency changes how you view daily tasks. You'll realize you're driving with angels, eating lunch with the Holy Spirit, and working at the office with Jesus. You may not see them, but, if you're reading your Bible, by faith you'll know they are present. People who have learned ways to stay connected to Heaven's frequency are operating in an enormous level of peace. No longer is this measure of glory reserved for a selected few. This is the hour for all Christians to step into God's promises. Let's make the Holy Spirit our best friend and ride His waves of peace.

Stormy Waters

> *When the disciples saw him walking on top of the water, they were terrified and screamed, "A ghost!"*
>
> *Then Jesus said, "Be brave and don't be afraid. I am here!"*

Peter shouted out, "Lord, if it's really you, then have me join you on the water!"

"Come and join me," Jesus replied. So Peter stepped out onto the water and began to walk toward Jesus. But when he realized how high the waves were, he became frightened and started to sink.

"Save me, Lord!" he cried out.

Jesus immediately stretched out his hand and lifted him up and said, "What little faith you have! Why would you let doubt win?" And the very moment they both stepped into the boat, the raging wind ceased.
(MATTHEW 14:26-32 TPT)

We have a decision. We can stay afraid in the boat or be at peace with Jesus out on the water. It goes against our instincts to put ourselves in harm's way, but it's actually the best choice. Our obedience is more important than safety. When we're afraid our instinct is to hide in our comfort zones where we can control our environment. Avoiding all of life's potential dangers will lead us to an unfulfilling existence. Cast off any fearful thoughts because they will lead to depression and anxiety. You weren't called to avoid the storm but to go through the storm.

Not only is Jesus telling us to step out from what's familiar, but to do what's impossible. Some call this *facing our fears*, but it's more like *keeping our face towards Jesus*. This is where peace is, right smack-dab in the middle of a storm. And if you want it, you must be willing to rest your feet on those angry seas without taking your eyes off of Jesus... not even for a second.

Peace through Prayer

Moments before Jesus stepped out onto the water, He had finished a several-hour prayer meeting alone with God. His encounter with Heaven left Him drenched in peace. Every inch of Him was covered with the oil of the Holy Spirit. And just like oil rests on top of water, Jesus walked on water with the anointing as His seal of protection. He was waterproof and stormproof. That's how He could step out onto crashing waves at 4 am. Even though it was pitch-black, windy, and wet, His peace came from tuning in to God. Jesus demonstrated how storms have little power over us when we're connected to Heaven.

Jesus told Peter, "Come and join me." Still, He is telling us to come and join Him. The only catch is we have to leave our comfort zones. Once Peter left the boat, he was leaving security. He had spent his life as a fisherman, so the boat was like a second home to him. When life gets rough, we have two choices: we will either default to our old attitude and securities, or step into the new and trust that Jesus knows what He's doing.

Peace in Trials

Peter walked on water as long as His eyes were on Jesus. He tapped into Jesus' anointing, when he believed. I wonder what would've happened if Peter hadn't lost his focus. How would it have played out, if he had stayed afloat? Perhaps they would've walked to the other side of the lake together. Or better yet, maybe they would've had fun jumping on the waves.

What a different story it would've been, if they had raced on the water or danced in the rain. Can you picture the rest of the disciples coming out to join the fun? After a while of amusement, I imagine the boat would've been a forgotten memory. For our entire lives, we're taught to look at trials as terrible things. But when we remained tuned in to Jesus, we're able to have fun in the trials.

Why didn't Jesus calm the storm before walking out onto the water? Why did He wait until He and Peter stepped back into the boat? He wanted to teach His disciples how to be unaffected by fear. What a wonderful lesson in faith and peace they could have learned. Instead, He realized they weren't ready, so He turned off the weather simulator. I'm sure He felt disappointed when they whined. He was going to show them such an amazing ability.

Usually when a storm in life hits, we beg God to turn it off. Sometimes He does. However, He'd rather see us endure the storm protected by the shield of faith, and maybe have a little fun while we're there.

Dancing on the Water

Is there a trial He can't handle? Each conquered storm in our lives proves God is faithful and will never leave us. Hard times will come. In fact, they come more often when we're living for God. This is our training for something greater. During a trial we may feel weakened, but, if we stay tuned in to God, we'll build spiritual grit. With His peace, we can live a life where nothing phases us because we know God has power over the storms. We can be unstoppable. Every tidal wave the enemy throws at us can become a joy ride. He can even sink our boat, and we'll dance on the water.

Peace vs. Fear

So we see that because of their unbelief they were not able to enter his rest.
(HEBREWS 3:19 NLT)

In this day and age, the word "anxiety" seems to run rampant. Even some Christians have adopted the term, "my anxiety," as if fear is another permanent appendage on their bodies. Have you ever read the symptoms of anxiety attacks? It sounds exactly like a page out of a demons and deliverance book. With the number of Christians on anxiety medication, we've got to ask ourselves, "why?" As the enemy increases his forces on the Earth, we must increase in Heaven's frequency. What used to work in the past won't have enough power for today.

The most dramatic result I've gained from tuning in to God is *peace*. Soaking in His presence has lifted fear off of me. Before I learned to seek God this way, I felt spiritually asleep. I still prayed and read the Word, yet attacks of fear increased. Life was getting tougher because the world was getting darker. This meant I needed to get brighter.

My old quiet times weren't cutting it. So, I got serious. I determined to remain connected to Heaven's frequency every moment of the day. Staying tuned in to God has kept the enemy tuned out. People may say staying in God's presence is too much work, but this is the way to abundant life. Would *you* want to go back to a life of pain and fear?

The Anointed Ones

> *Do not touch my anointed ones;*
> *do my prophets no harm.*
> *(PSALMS 105:15 NIV)*

It's certain we will have trials, but the Holy Spirit will shield us if we allow Him. Like the ten wise virgins, our time in His presence will give us the oil of the Holy

Spirit, which acts as a seal of protection. Like an invisible barrier, His anointing keeps us unharmed. We can trust He's in control, even when death is staring us down. So, sit back, relax, and watch the enemy throw his hissy fit. There's nothing he can do to us because God says, *"Don't touch them!"*

If *love* is the frequency of the presence of God, then *faith* is the frequency of the anointing. We receive the anointing through faith. We must believe beyond all doubt who we are and who Jesus is, so the anointing can protect us. The truth of God's Word will build our shields of faith. If we doubt God is big enough to handle things, then as a result, we cultivate belief in the enemy's power. Let's not allow fear to weaken the protection over our lives. We must trust God. Once we give God control, we'll be shielded with the anointing of the Holy Spirit.

Inner and outer Anointing

There's a difference between the anointing on the inside of us and the anointing on the outside of us. I often wondered why I only felt God's presence powerfully at certain church services. I was overwhelmed by God's immense glory at the Brownsville Revival and in other meetings where anointed preachers ministered. The power they carried came from a life saturated with the Kingdom of Heaven. Outwardly, I was feeling their anointing. When I walked away, I felt it for a few days, but it wasn't lasting. Since I spent little of my day in God's presence, I didn't have the same measure of anointing inside me.

Today, I frequently seek Heaven, and the anointing inside me is increasing. The same level of glory I felt at the revivals is now burning in my heart. Just last night, I woke up shaking under the power of the Holy Spirit. This has become my new normal! I don't require a service or minister to be overwhelmed with Heaven; I experience it every day. As amazing as my experiences have been, I know this is only the fringes of His glory.

Fountains

I recently had a vision of a refreshing rain covering the Earth. It was during the worldwide crisis with COVID-19, and this vision encouraged me. I was sitting at my piano and began singing, "*Let it rain, let it rain, open the windows of Heaven.*" God stopped me with a second vision. A massive fountain was before me. Its waters were bursting through the atmosphere and falling as a gentle rain. Zooming out, I saw there were many fountains causing this global rain. Each fountain was inside a Christian, and their prayers and worship were gushing out like water, quenching the dry earth.

God corrected me. I didn't need to ask for the windows of Heaven to open because He had a better plan. He said, "Rain from Heaven was My *visitation*, but this rain is My *habitation*." I believe God wants to bless our land, and He prefers to work through His children.

In the past there were rainy seasons of His glory. These were temporary visitations of revival. A permanent habitation means His people will remain tuned in to Heaven's frequency. We won't need the windows of Heaven to open because the Kingdom of Heaven will rule and reign through us.

Habitation

This is our cue. He is looking for those who He can inhabit with the Kingdom of Heaven. They must become soaked with the love of God and relinquish control to the Holy Spirit. We've sat back and watched moves of God long enough. This is our generation. This is our turn. We only have one shot to make it count. The world is crying out for Christians who will bring the Kingdom of Heaven to them. We must allow God to take us through the trials because our training time is coming to an end. Right now, He's calling the oil-saturated believers out of their boats and onto the water. Will you step out?

Final Note

Jesus replied, "Every plant not planted by my Heavenly Father will be uprooted."
(MATTHEW 15:2 NLT)

It's in our design to be a habitation of God's glory. From before the beginning of time, we were in Him. He sent us to Earth as He breathed life into our physical beings and placed a destiny in our hearts. He planned how we would look and crafted our personalities to be unique, and it pleased Him. How excited He was to see us take our first breath and begin our journey on this Earth. It was bitter sweet when He released us. He hoped we would choose to come back, but sadly so many children have forgotten Him.

Oh, the joy He has over the ones who love Him. He knows they will one day reign with Him for eternity, never to be apart again. Eagerly, He waits for the day to be united with them in Heaven.

In the meantime, there are those wild children of His who can't wait. They spend their lives seeking Him even though they are still in their earthly bodies. The enemy can't hurt them and circumstances don't seem to scare them because their faith is unwavering. Every evil tactic is futile.

These warriors are set on fire by the Holy Spirit for the purpose of pushing back the darkness. They know there's treasure in the secret place, and nothing will stop them in their pursuit. These children are sealed as the lovers of God. He doesn't need to wait another day to be with them because they stay connected to Him on Heaven's frequency.

Bibliography

Hibbert, Albert. *Smith Wigglesworth: The Secret of His Power*. Asheville, NC: Harrison House, LLC, 1982.

Oxford University Press. "Definition of Romance Noun." Oxford's Learner's Dictionaries. Oxford University Press, 2020. www.oxfordlearnersdictionaries.com/us/

Sensory Trust. "5,9,21,53... How Many Senses Do We Have?" Sensory Trust. Sensory Trust Organization, 2020. www.sensorytrust.org.uk.